Saint Mary's School, Ascot

Saint Mary's School, Ascot and its Antecedents

ROY WAKE

HAGGERSTON PRESS
London

Published by The Haggerston Press
38 Kensington Place, London w8 7PR

**All orders to the Bursar,
St Mary's School Ascot, SL5 9JF**

Printed in Great Britain
at The Bath Press, Avon

1 869812 11 5

Contents

Illustrations

Mlle Arlette Kalflèche
Mrs Rhian Amery
Mrs Clare Davies
Group Captain Philip Callan
Sister Mark Orchard as a novice
Sister Mark in a hard hat
Sister Mark (now Sister Frances), 1994
The development of the School buildings

Colour reproductions of eight of the paintings from the "Painted Life of Mary Ward" will be found between pp 24 and 25.

Foreword

The Governors asked Roy Wake to write a history of the school because it is important for us all to appreciate St Mary's Ascot through its history and evolution. This he has done with insight and a special understanding of the contribution that the IBVM has made to Catholic education. Sadly, today, there are fewer Sisters in the Province than, say, fifty years ago, and fewer still committed to the school apostolate. The decision by the IBVM to set up an independent board of governors, and to hand over to it the running of the school, was fully in keeping with the Second Vatican Council; it shewed the concern of the IBVM with the future good of the school. A Trust has been established whose responsibility will be to maintain the close connection between the Institute and the school in the years to come, and to make sure that the ethos of the school – the vision of Mary Ward and her companions which Roy recounts in his history – remains for ever at its core.

The Governors make no apologies for the high quality of education they are helping to provide. They are only partners in a large enterprise, in which all the Headmistresses, teachers and ancillary staff have participated over the years, and indeed the Governors are justifiably proud of the present state of this partnership.

The pursuit of excellence is a necessary part of any Christian ideal, and it is quite possible to enter into a competition of excellence whilst at the same time loving, helping, and respecting one's competitors. We are asked by Christ to make the best possible use of our God-given talents, and St Mary's helps those in its care to do so. But, however clearly committed the school will always be to the ideals of educational excellence, its Catholic foundation also commits it to the highest ideals of pastoral care for each pupil; this is a dimension of school life not easily measured by publishable results.

The possible vulnerability of each child must never be ignored. Our task is to help young children to flourish in this community where the love of learning and the desire for God can be found together.

The decision by the IBVM to appoint Sister Gillian Orchard to a special Chaplaincy in all their schools has already brought great benefit to St Mary's Ascot. She is helping staff and Governors to draw on their spiritual reserves, and to develop their understanding that the ministry of education in the Church belongs to all – lay, religious and clerical. The appointment of Fr Dermot Power as School Chaplain has refreshed the spiritual life of the school and complements Sister Gillian's work. The old community of Sisters has passed, but we are making great efforts, by building accommodation on the estate, to bring lay staff into a new community. The Governors are committed to the belief that whatever changes are to be faced they must always be in the spirit of Mary Ward and her Institute.

JOHN ALBERT
Chairman of the Governing Board

We are but Women . . . Women may be perfect and fervour must not necessarily decay because we are women. Women may be perfect as well as men if they love verity and seek true knowledge . . . It is not learning that I commend to you but knowledge, true knowledge which you all may have if you love and seek it.

From the Second Instruction of Mary Ward, c.1618

Introduction

For if heaven be on this earth, and ease to any soul,
It is in cloister or in school, by many skills I find.
LANGLAND: *Piers Plowman*

This book is about an independent school. As formerly one of Her Majesty's Inspectors of Schools, with responsibility for many notable independent schools, I think I know all the arguments against private, fee-paying schooling, but I find none of them offers a convincing reason why people should not be free to spend their properly earned money as they wish. If they care to spend it on cars, holidays, horse-racing, comfortable housing, even buying their council houses, that is their affair, and we should not legislate against it. By no means are all the parents in fee-paying schools wealthy; many make sacrifices for something which they hold to be good. There are Assisted Places, and most schools have bursary schemes to enable pupils from less well-off families to make the move, though sometimes there are difficulties in the transition. I have heard Ascot denigrated as a school for rich Catholic girls, but this is not a generalisation that holds true. Until ten years ago, the fees were very low because an institute of women Religious served it without payment; only the increasing number of lay staff has required a proper fee structure.

As for privilege, to grow up in a home that possesses books is to be advantaged against those who do not; to be a member of a family in which adults and adolescents continue to talk with each other is a great advantage over those who do not or cannot; one could go on producing examples, all shewing the very large number of gradations in privilege. Divisiveness is put forward as a very strong argument, but good neighbourhoods divide from bad. No school, anywhere, has a complete social mix. One of the most shallow cases argued for the compulsory comprehensive school was that it would obviate or ameliorate all kinds of divisions. A reasonable working knowledge of such schools would soon destroy such illusions. Our society is, at present, in muddled retreat from many of the strongly held positions indicated here.

This book is an attempt not only to recount the history of St Mary's Ascot, and place that history in context, but also to shew that it has been a thoroughly defensible, responsible and praise-worthy educational venture. The school has stressed that privilege itself brings responsibility, not only of service, but of leadership. There is plenty of evidence that present-day senior girls, and Old Girls of all generations, have tried to serve God, the Church and the world in all kinds of ways, from the most private, to work in the full public glare. Sometimes the phrase "Catholic Guilt" occurs when talking to them, but this in truth is no more than shorthand for a sense of how much there is to be done, and how different people can find different ways of doing it.

Some readers may well wonder how and why it came about that I, of all people, was asked by the Governors to write a history of St Mary's School at Ascot. After all, I have not been a parent or a teacher there; I have not had a long association with the school or with the Institute of the Blessed Virgin Mary. My relationship with it began only in the May of 1983. In the previous year, Sister M. Emmanuel (now Sister Gillian Orchard), was relieved of the head-ship because of serious illness and her own sister, Sister M. Mark, was put in her place, taking over in the September of 1982. The new Head felt acutely her lack of experience and of perspective, and therefore she sought for a general appraisal of the school. The Catholic Education Council accepted her invitation, and for some days in May 1983 carried out a team visit, led by Norbert Winstan-ley, its secondary advisor. I knew Norbert from other work, and he invited me to join the visit, which I did on the 18th and 19th of May. The reasons for Norbert's invitation to me were firstly that I was a senior member of H. M. Inspectorate of Schools with a national responsibility for secondary education, secondly because I was a

Catholic, thirdly because I was unable to discover on whose list in the Inspectorate the school was. The school file took some finding, and I realised that St Mary's had, so to speak, been forgotten or had slipped through somebody's net. In these circumstances, it was simplest and most sensible to take up the file myself. So began an unbroken association with the school from that day onwards (at any rate until this book is published).

The visit by Norbert Winstanley's team was not an inspection in the formal sense, but rather a series of individual conversations, mostly confidential, with members of staff, brought together in a general examination of aims, methods, and of over-all management. Discussion with Sister Mark took place all through the visit, with a concluding session followed up by a detailed written report. One copy of this was sent to the Marble Arch Trust, as it was known then.

The Trust had helped Sister Mark to instigate the whole exercise, not least because financial control was involved and advice needed in this field. It became clear that the school had reached a critical point in its history. Amongst the many recommendations was one that the IBVM should take steps towards the formation of an independent governing body, to which the Institute should hand over the affairs of the school. The headmistress should be a member, the Institute should be present as governors and trustees, and of course would remain the owner of all the property. Essentially, however, the new governors were to be Catholic lay people. (At the time of writing this, the board consists of ten lay Governors, with three members of the Institute. The Institute continues to own the whole property, acting through trustees, two of whom sit on the board.) As soon as possible, a professional bursar was to be appointed, to take in hand the finances of the school, and the management and maintenance of all the buildings of the estate.

The IBVM accepted these findings and moved quickly to establish such a board, with Julian Bell as the first Chairman. It met for the first time on September 7th 1984. By then I had left the Inspectorate, and so was able to accept the invitation to join the board. A new and increasingly spectacular period in the school's history began, and it was from a justifiable pride in what has happened that the governors wanted the whole story of the school's life re-told and brought up to date. An added edge to it is that, whether we like the prospect or not, and we do not, there may be another and even more dramatic point looming up, namely the handing over to lay headship.

I am the outsider looking in. This book follows and records my own journey of discovery. I cannot claim original research, but I have done a great deal of talking with people and as much reading as possible. I have tried sympathetically to understand not simply the school, but the Institute from which it sprang, and something of the great personalities in the story.

There is a gentle and charming story, told by Kenneth Rose in his biography of George V, about Princess Mary Adelaide, Duchess of Teck, grand-daughter of George III and mother of Queen Mary—a large, good-natured, much-loved lady who was almost always in debt. Her debts became legendary. "At a time when tradesmen were pressing her for the payment of bills amounting to almost twenty thousand pounds (in the 1880s), she was invited to open a new church hall in Kensington, to which John Barker, the grocer, had contributed handsomely. 'And now', she told her audience, 'I must propose a special vote of thanks to Mr Barker, to whom we owe so much'."

I owe so much to many people, in particular to Mrs Audrey Atter, with whom I developed a method in which I did the talking and she did the work; this became, in time, a partnership central to the genesis of the book. I hope that the list that now follows, of the names of other people to whom I am greatly indebted, is fully inclusive because, as the text of the book makes clear, I have had to rely on oral evidence to a much greater extent than I expected. The documentary evidence for St Mary's School is slender and rather monotonous. The list of people who have given their time in talking to me, and in many cases, in writing about their personal memories and reflections, is very considerable.

Firstly there is Sister Mark. Since I began to write the book, she went away on a year's sabbatical, during which she decided to use her own name; therefore she is now Sister M. Frances Orchard. Secondly, I have been helped, and guided, by Sister Gillian, who was Sister Emmanuel; the first Appendix, on the Painted Life, is entirely her work, and she has advised me on all matters concerning the history of the IBVM. Sister M. Pia Buxton, the Provincial of the English Province, has given me much information, not least about the three branches of the Institute, and agreed most kindly to write Appendix Two, on the General Congregation that took place in the summer of 1993, bringing all the Provincials and their advisors, from all over the world, to Ascot. The Bursar, Group Captain Philip Callan, has helped me in so many ways, and particularly in writing about his years as the first bursar in the school's history. I have been supported at every turn by Mrs Clare Davies, the headmistress's secretary and devoted servant of the school.

Amongst Old Girls, I have been received kindly, and indeed entertained, by Mrs Catherine Devas/Nolan, Lady Antonia Fraser/Pakenham, the Hon. Mrs Olga Polizzi/Forte, Miss Marina Warner and the Hon. Mrs Sarah Hogg/Boyd-Carpenter. To continue the list: Sister Lavinia Byrne; Sister Bridget Geoffrey-Smith; Sister Magdalen Ingram; Sister Isabelle McIrvine; Sister Gregory Kirkus; Sister Agatha Leach; Sister Michaela Robinson; Mr J. M. Beveridge, the nephew of Mother Ignatius; Mrs Rhian Amery (acting headmistress, 1993 to 1994) and many members of the staff of the school; Julian Bell (the first Chairman of the Governors); Fr Ian Ker; Mrs Cathune Cape/Johnston; Mrs Kisielewska Dunbar/O'Donnell; Miss Amelia FitzAlan Howard; Lady Deirdre McNair Wilson/Tuckett; Miss Bella Pack; and present pupils of the school.

I

Mary Ward and the Institute of the Blessed Virgin Mary

Reverend Mothers and Mistresses of Discipline may come and go, but their characters affect the school very little. The real ruler is an invisible one . . . the Foundress.

ANTONIA WHITE: 'A Child of the Five Wounds', an essay in *The Old School*, a collection edited by Graham Greene, 1934

How far this quotation by Antonia White about her own school days at the Convent of the Sacred Heart at Roehampton is applicable to St Mary's or not, will be unfolded in the narrative. The chronological development from the foundation of the school in 1885 must be recorded, and personalities recalled, keeping in mind another quotation, which I have used often in a teaching life, from Maeterlinck's *Bluebird*: "There are no dead" (it meant so much to that most sensitive medieval historian Eileen Power). But these would still only make for a limited story, which is why it has to be a history in context.

In the first place, it is the story of a girls' Catholic school, moreover a boarding school, and one established and directed by a religious order; in other words, it is about a convent boarding school. Under all these headings, emotions can be aroused. Loyalty, love, gratitude, dislike, bitter reaction to much convent school education, are more than enough to have provided the material for a sizeable collection of books. The argument takes in whether there should be boarding education, and has brought religious orders into internal division about involvement in the education of fee-paying children, thereby becoming caught up in the matter of vocations, or the lack of them, to such orders. It is now leading to disputes about whether there should be separate denominational schooling at all. For good measure, you can add the emotions stirred up by the trend towards admitting girls into boys' schools, most obviously at sixth-form level, but also co-education generally. St Mary's Ascot has been variously affected by these issues.

Mary Ward was the foundress of the only religious English Order or Congregation for women in the Church's history. The school is part of the life and history of the English Province of that Apostolic Institute, the Institute of the Blessed Virgin Mary, and, until the establishment of the governing board, the Institute, through the Superiors at Ascot and the Provincials who lived on the same estate, controlled every aspect of its life. Unless one can capture something of the essence of the IBVM, its heart and spirituality even more than its history, then to record the story of the school itself would be a comparatively minor affair.

I was profoundly affected to discover that it was only in 1703 that Pope Clement XI, in the Papal Brief *Inscrutabili*, approved a Rule for the Institute, giving it thereby a name by which it could be known, the Institute of Mary, but on the strictest condition that no claim should be made that Mary Ward was its Foundress. It set me on the track to finding and appreciating in ever greater degree the person-ality and purposes of one of the most extraordinary women in the history of the Church.

On my first visit to the school, I saw and asked about a series of painted panels that I was told were part of what is called "The Painted Life". These record events in the life of Mary Ward. The Ascot panels are copies; the originals are in the Provincialate in Augsburg. I saw also a large framed photograph of a serene old lady. I was told that she was Mother Cecilia Marshall, whose biography, written by Father Corbishley SJ, I borrowed. So I began to grasp something of her achievement also. The obvious task was to link the two, and to begin to penetrate the story that connected them. The best general introduction to the former that I found was *Till God Will—Mary Ward through her writings*, compiled and edited by

Sister M. Emmanuel Orchard in 1985. Its bibliography refers to five sets of original documents, after which there has not been very much secondary writing until recently. The chief book in English was undoubtedly *The Life of Mary Ward, 1585-1645*, in two volumes, 1882 and 1885, by Mother M. Catherine Chambers. She, in fact, was a companion of Mother Joseph Edwards (whose portrait hangs opposite to Cecilia Marshall's photograph) in bringing the Sisters to Ascot.

The great resurgence of interest in Mary Ward came as a result of the work of the Second Vatican Council, whose avowed purpose was to renew and reinvigorate the life of the Church. The decree *Perfectae Caritatis*, of the 28th October 1965 was addressed to all religious orders and congregations, but it had a particular and peculiar significance for the IBVM. It required that all orders should undertake a thorough examination of themselves. This was to be done, following these general principles: a return to the sources, and a requirement that the orders should modify and adapt their ways to ensure that they met the needs of our times. In more detail, the sources were indicated as: the Gospels, the spirit of the founder, and the tested and proven sound traditions of each order. Then, taking the matter further, came the decree *Ecclesiae Sanctae* of 6th August 1966. This required a detailed revision of the general laws or constitutions of every order or congregation by its highest authority, after a full and ample consultation with all its members. The results were not to be simply juridical in character, but rather to express the evangelical and theological principles concerning their religious life, and its place in the life of the whole Church. The Council wanted an apt and accurate formulation in which the spirit and aims of the founder should be clearly recognised, faithfully preserved, and given new life. This brought the whole matter of Mary Ward, the foundress, forcefully back into the heart of study and discussion in the IBVM. Such calls for a return to sources, or first principles, to renewal and the release of new energies were a central part of the work of the Council. Pope John XXIII wanted breezes, even winds, to blow through every orchard in the life of the Church;

but often the boughs trembled, and fruit fell off. Many people were excited, many disturbed, and some dismayed. Some even claimed that "the faithful would hardly notice the changes". I was myself assured of this by Cardinal Heenan. I did not believe him, but I do not matter. The faith of someone like Evelyn Waugh (an Ascot parent), who did matter, was tested to the limit, and for him, and many another, all joy and mystery departed from the Church; faith dimmed, and Church attendance became a duty.

Different orders and congregations took up these challenges at different paces, with different styles; some quite publicly, many discreetly among themselves. The English Benedictine Congregation published *Consider Your Call* in 1978, a penetrating and far-reaching scrutiny of every aspect of its life, nonetheless radical for being so mildly written. The IBVM got down to the task first in 1968, but mainly in the 1970s, so that the spirit of unrest that all such re-visitations seem to have caused was felt in that decade, rather than earlier. There is, so far as I can gather, no publication illuminating this full review of all the rules of the Institute. Certainly there is no pocket rule book; there never has been. The Institute came out of the Spiritual Exercises of St Ignatius, and then from the Jesuit Constitutions. Essentially speaking, the unrest came out of how the rediscovery of Mary Ward affected different members of the Institute.

Rediscovery may be rather like cleaning a picture, and the results may be quite startling. Freshness can bring immediacy, and the centuries fall away. It is, as I have found, no small task to disentangle the history of the Institute, to get back to Mary Ward herself and her first companions. She was born in 1585, near Ripon. Her family and all her relations were part of a close network of Catholic recusants held together by their womenfolk. Her own sisters became nuns; one brother became a Jesuit, and the other was killed in a duel, so there are no direct descendants of the family. When Mary Ward was one year old, Margaret Clitherow was judicially murdered in York, for her recusant faith, on Good Friday 1586, which in that year was also the Feast of the Annunciation. "She was laid flat on the ground, tied up half-naked in the form of a cross between two doors, with a great sharpened stone in the small of her back; and then she was crushed to death." She was pregnant. This happened near Ouse Bridge. Mary Ward's family and relations, all Yorkshire people, lived increasingly isolated from the national and local life of late sixteenth and early seventeenth-century England. In the eyes of the government, they were traitors or potential traitors, and if they were harried, or arrested and imprisoned, or put to death, it was as such.

Pope Innocent III (1198-1216), in his determination to exalt the power of the Papacy, had extended its claims to embrace not only spiritual but also secular power, putting the See of Peter at the head of the political and religious life of Christendom. All his successors claimed this "Plenitudo Potestatis", the right and the duty to regulate the affairs of kings and princes. By this right, therefore, Pius V issued the Bull, *Regnans in Excelsis* in 1570, to "declare the aforesaid Elizabeth a heretic and an abettor of heretics . . . we declare her to be deprived of her pretended right to the aforesaid realm [England] . . . and the nobles, subjects and peoples of the said realm . . . we declare to be absolved for ever from all dues of . . . fidelity and obedience . . . and we deprive the said Elizabeth of her pretended right to the realm." The Government retaliated with increasingly severe legislation, culminating in the Act against Recusants of 1593, effectively classifying Catholics as traitors "hiding their most detestable and devilish purposes under a false pretext of religion and conscience". In fact, most Catholics saw themselves as loyal English people, and had to live in the most testing of dilemmas. They prayed (as we still do) for the return of England to the old faith, but they were not traitors. After all, Elizabeth's chief naval commander against the Spanish Armada was Lord Howard of Effingham, a Catholic.

A major irony in Mary Ward's life was that it had to be lived mostly abroad, that her endeavours first took root there, but that during all her life she saw herself as working for her own country; and at the last, she died just outside York on January 20th 1645, O. S., now January 30th, N. S. She wanted to give her life entirely to God, but found that she could not accept the only pattern that the

Church offered to women Religious, that of the enclosed life. She was gripped by the desire for an uncluttered freedom to serve the Church by enhancing the dignity of women. She became certain that Divine illumination showed her that she was not to be a Poor Clare or a Carmelite.

There seems to have been a deep fear of women and female sexuality running through medieval Catholicism, and by no means dead in the Counter-Reformation period. For instance, when a distinctive religious development started in late-medieval Flanders, namely the formation of communities separately of men and women, usually middle-aged but not necessarily so, who simply decided to live in common, it aroused great suspicion and resentment. They lived either in adjacent houses or, as time went by, in purpose-built clusters; they followed no rule, had no structure of authority, were in no way an Order, and were not under episcopal control. One of the names given them—"béguine"—was derived from "Albigensian", shewing a popular suspicion of heresy, and of spreading secret societies. Women in particular attracted great hostility. Starting in Liège, the movement spread throughout the Low Countries. There was much male fury at the mere idea of groups of self-supporting women, living holy lives that certainly were celibate—and refusing to marry; Canon Law did not recognise widowhood as a valid status before sixty. At its height this was a very considerable movement. There was—and still is (though it is now lived in by Benedictine nuns) a Béguinage in Bruges; only in the 1930s did the last Béguines give up the place. One of their main forms of livelihood was lace-making, and the area still has a large number of shops selling lace.

Ecclesiastical and lay authority felt secure only if men and women were married or in clearly defined enclosed orders; even St Clare was never remotely able to establish a Franciscan Second Order with the freedom to wander the earth that the friars had. When Mary Ward decided that this was not the life for her, she stepped out into a climate fraught with deepest suspicion. Contemporary society could not begin to envisage and accept the idea of

The Painted Life: 4 Mary Ward saved from a fire at her family home, aged 10

9 Told of persecutions and punishments, she resolves to enter the religious life

13 She cannot be persuaded to marry

14 An incident at mass persuades a priest to help her

21 A vision shows that she is not to be an enclosed nun

27 Mary Ward with her first companions

27 She is convinced all who work selflessly in the Institute will be saved

30 Her special vocation to be with ordinary people of all kinds

freely travelling, unenclosed women Religious; dressing as widows would not get them out of that problem. It was at this point that Mary Ward received the guidance she needed, but which never made for an easy life.

> Some other thing was determined for me, without all comparison more to the glory of God . . . I did not see what the assured good thing would be, but the glory of God which was to come through it, showed itself inexplicably and so abundantly as to fill my soul . . . Great instance was made by divers spiritual and learned men that we would take upon us some Rule already confirmed . . . but, they seemed not that which God would have done . . . About this time in the year 1611, I fell sick in great extremity but being somewhat recovered, I went according to a vow made, in pilgrimage . . . Being alone in some extraordinary repose of mind I heard distinctly, not by sound of voice, but intellectually understood, these words: Take the Same of the Society—so understood as that we were to take the same both in matter and manner, that only excepted which God, by diversity of sex prohibited . . . All is as done by me; it only remains that I be faithful on my part.

"The Society" was the Society of Jesus—the Jesuits—whose constitution Mary Ward saw as the only one that would serve her purposes. So began the continuous links with St Ignatius Loyola's Exercises and Constitutions. She and her followers were to be flattered and insulted by being called Jesuitesses. Years of negotiation in Rome, and the most extraordinary journeys, often on foot, were spent in trying to get Papal approval. The opposition of many cardinals and bishops in the end nullified the warm support she had received, at first, from Pope Urban VIII. Her period of growing success, which had begun in 1609 in St Omer, and then in 1616 with the establishment of a pattern of schools from Liège, to Cologne and Trèves in 1621, to Naples and Rome in 1623, Perugia in 1624, Munich and Vienna in 1627, Pressburg in 1628, came to an end in that year with a Decree of Propaganda to suppress "the Jesuitesses". In 1631 came the Bull: *Pastoralis Romani Pontificis*, which condemned and banned the Institute.

It has to be stressed that Mary Ward lived the second half of her life at a time when war, of ever-increasing and eventually unparalleled savagery, began to afflict central Europe. The tensions that were described as religious, building up between Catholics, Lutherans and Calvinists, burst out on May 23rd 1618, with the Defenestration of Prague—an episode that has always enthralled schoolchildren, because it is the only time that the word is used in English history books, though there were other defenestrations, and at least one depontification in Bohemia. But the event—the throwing out from an upper window of representatives of the Holy Roman Emperor by Protestant envoys—was not intrinsically funny. The war that then began raged over Western Europe for thirty years, bringing some famous episodes such as the establishment, briefly, of Sweden as a major power, when it had a population of no more than one and a half million. The idea that it was a war fought under religious banners and for religious creeds became as farcical as applying the same idea to present-day Northern Ireland, but it produced destruction and depopulation on a scale not even surpassed by the Black Death, and came to an end only in 1648 with the signing of the Treaty of Westphalia (the last international treaty to be written in Latin). Bertold Brecht's play, *Mother Courage*, powerfully brings out the chaos, the muddle, the treachery and the hypocrisy of this time. It was in this world that Mary Ward and her companions, especially Mary Poyntz, achieved the setting up of houses and schools, chiefly because of the protection of the Catholic Elector of Bavaria, and his links with Hapsburg Flanders.

When Mary Ward returned to England in 1639, it was to the tensions that led to the outbreak of civil war in 1642. I suppose she was inherently royalist, and was in her native York when it was besieged and captured by Parliamentary forces, managing to escape to a nearby village, where she died. It is important to keep these matters in mind when recording her travels and achievements—also to keep in mind that this small group of women learnt to work, to argue and to defend themselves in Latin, French, German and Italian.

To the IBVM and to any sensible historian the history of the Institute is of the acorn to oak-tree type, that is of continuous organic growth, an evolutionary development from all that Mary Ward intended and achieved. For the purposes of survival, the Institute has had to go along with the fiction that Mary Ward's original work ended in the January of 1631, so that what she herself did for the rest of her life, and the work of her companions after her death, has had to be regarded, in this fiction, as a completely new and separate history. The only way in which Abbot Gasquet, and those working with him in the early years of the pontificate of Pius X, could persuade Cardinal Merry del Val to take up the "cause" of the Institute, in order to establish at long last that Mary Ward was indeed its Foundress, was to claim—or pretend—that a new religious congregation, "carefully avoiding all the features that had been forbidden and under a reformed way of life", dated from after 1631. The Plea said that "It is quite certain that there was no intention of reviving the Institute condemned by Urban VIII; this Congregation of English Ladies must be regarded as quite new, wholly different from the one which had been suppressed once and for all."

It was this fictitious, new Institute that Clement XI had recognised in 1703. It was given no name then, but by 1707, it was tacitly known as the Institute of Mary, and from 1714, this was the usage in the vow formula. The Papal wriggling and equivocating continued, finding "for reasons of prudence" that this new Institute could not recognise Mary Ward as Foundress "whom they had hitherto been accustomed to call their originator". The final wriggle said that this prohibition, necessary for reasons of prudence, "was clearly not of such a nature as to determine anything about a matter of history". Abbot Gasquet, whose general reputation as an historian was mangled by one of my tutors, G. G. Coulton, nevertheless served the English Ladies well, and persuaded the Holy See, in some fine flowery language, effectively to drop this nonsense so that "now that circumstances are entirely different there is nothing to prevent the

Institute of the B.V.M. commonly called that of the English Ladies, from being able to acknowledge, even in public, that Mary Ward is their Foundress". Even then, the statement had resoundingly to conclude: "having due regard to the decrees of the Holy See concerning all other matters and disregarding everything to the contrary". Make of that what you will.

The Bull of 1631 led to Mary Ward's imprisonment for a time and, even after her release, overshadowed the rest of her life. Her work had to be conducted in the shadows. How could the Institute escape such a severe and total condemnation of its Foundress? There followed the tangled story of Roman and clerical hostility, and yet there was also the personal warmth of Urban VIII, so obviously disregarded by his own cardinals. In the Introduction to her two-volume *Life*, Mother Catherine Chambers examined and underlined the many reasons why Mary Ward's proposals aroused such immense hostility. Not only had other attempts to create free-moving unenclosed companies of female Religious failed—she quotes the early Ursulines—but also, apparently, St Ignatius himself had warned his companions against getting involved with attempts to found similar organisations.

> It is certain that, however eager individual Fathers, acquainted with a particular Congregation of women and interested in their work, might be to further its interests in every possible way, the weight of the authority of the Society would be thrown into the scale against the new institution, on the simple ground of the resolute determination of St Ignatius to exempt his children from the burthen of alliances of this kind. And it is even more certain that the Society would never, as a body, take an active part in furthering such a scheme . . . If the Society, as distinguished from individual Fathers, was certain to oppose her plan, it was certain also to be opposed by the enemies of the Society . . . A new proposal would be looked upon by its many jealous enemies as an indirect attempt to increase its influence.

She goes on to castigate pretty fiercely the divisions amongst English Catholics that also hindered Mary Ward's work in her own country—"which made the Catholic body at that time the tool and laughing stock of its enemies, and the source of the most poignant grief to its friends". She takes her case further with the challenging statement that "when the great Day of Account shall reveal all secrets, it will perhaps be seen that the dissensions amongst the English Catholics did more to prevent the restoration of the ancient faith in the country, than the Anglican Establishment and the persecuting Government of which that Establishment has always been the subservient tool". Good strong stuff in these ecumenical days.

On the Continent, secular rulers in the Imperial lands, especially in Flanders and Bavaria, did see the immeasurable value of schools for girls, so that often the Sisters were able to survive in a sort of underground way. It can be maintained however that, in a strict sense, Mary Ward achieved nothing permanent in her lifetime. She had been condemned for heresy, schism and disobedience, massive charges that blighted the Institute until modern times—hence the embarrassment referred to already. I have failed to find out what heresy she was accused of. The truth is that, quite simply, she affronted a male world that was scandalised by what they saw as her outrageous pretensions. In return, she was outraged by male comment. Among the last recorded talks that she gave are the "Verity" talks, at St Omer in 1617. They were sparked off by the following incidents:

> While Mr Sackville was commending us . . . Father Minister, who was present, answered: "It is true, while they are in their first fervour, but fervour decays, and when all is done, they are but women. Fervour not being in the feelings." She said, "but in a will to do well which women may have as well as men. There is no such difference between men and women. Yet women, may they not do great matter? . . . I hope in God that it will be seen that women, in time to come, will do much . . . I would to God

that all men understood this truth. Women, if they will, may be perfect, and if they would not make us believe that we can do nothing and we are 'but women', we might do great matters . . . I must still say that it is not truth, but a lie, to say that fervour must necessarily decay, that we are 'but women' . . . Now sisters, since God has particularly looked upon you, calling you to this state of life and giving you this vocation, I doubt not that some of you thirst greatly after the effecting of His will."

These talks are profoundly moving and they establish, for me and many others, her greatness and her courage. She saw that the most obvious way to carry out her mission was to offer a quality and range of education to girls that had never been offered before. It is a most intriguing question as to where her educational thinking came from. In the recusant Yorkshire world, women certainly were immensely important, but essentially and precisely as mothers and heads of families. They provided stability, and often a great deal of defiance to the Protestant authorities; they were literate, and well-read in devotional books. They were prayerful, they were pillars of strength, but their educational range was obviously limited. John Bossy, in his book, *The English Catholic Community 1570 to 1850*, makes much of this point.

> The average woman of the (Catholic) upper classes might reasonably feel that the Reformation had not been designed with her in mind. If she was married a whole sequence of ritual functions had been removed from her jurisdiction by the decline of fasting and abstinence and desacralisation of Holydays; if she was not, she had lost the chance of an honourable and possibly useful life in a religious order . . . All in all, I think the evidence entitles us to conclude that, to a considerable degree the Catholic community owed its existence to gentlewomen's dissatisfaction with the Reformation settlement of religion, and that they played an abnormally important part in its early history.

Yet we find that Mary Ward referred to the need for girls to be far more than this, to be knowledgeable in the "liberal arts". This refers, undoubtedly, to the "trivium" and "quadrivium" of the medieval universities—grammar (that is, Latin), rhetoric (that is, the ability to think clearly and to argue), logic, music, arithmetic, geometry, astronomy. The only proper guess is that she first learnt about these from the Jesuit priests who travelled in disguise around the recusant world, and they were confirmed in her by her close association with the Jesuits at St Omer.

When Mary Ward first left England in 1606, she joined a convent of the Poor Clares, which she shortly left to establish a new one especially for English women to come to join. (This convent continued after she had left it, and in the 19th century returned to Darlington.) Still unconvinced that this was the true path for her, she returned to England in 1609, under private vow, to work amongst poor Catholics in London. Soon she gathered around her a group of like-minded young women—they who are portrayed in what we know as number 22 in the Painted Life—who returned to St Omer, and gained permission from the local bishop to start schools for the townsfolk and for English exiles. In 1611, she was seriously ill with measles, and on her recovery went on pilgrimage to a local shrine. It was there that she received the illumination to align herself with the Ignatian life, and she began a close association with exiled Jesuits, particularly Fr Roger Lee. This did not make for easier relationships with the recusant secular priests trained for the English Mission at Douai. The Douai Seminary had, to start with, taken in some boys whose first education had been with the Jesuits, but relationships between the secular clergy in exile and the Jesuits were never easy. The dominant personality amongst the Jesuits was Fr Persons (or Parsons), whose great ambition was to create an English Jesuit Province, and for this purpose he wanted his own seminary. He obtained an annual grant of money from Philip II of Spain, and chose St Omer as his base because "no part thereof liked him better than the Low Countries in regard to their nearness to England and air most like unto the air of an English climate." In fact, St

Omer became a very considerable centre of English Catholic exiles, not least for nunneries, with which the Jesuits had close links. Mary Ward's first convent for the Poor Clares for English girls, already referred to, was started at St Omer. It moved to Gravelines. Indeed it was through the good offices of the Jesuits, and their links with the Archduchess Isabella, the Hapsburg Regent, that she was able to buy the land. T. E. Muir, in his *History of Stonyhurst College 1593–1993*, has written that "Under the guidance of Fr Roger Lee, who acted as their Chaplain, they even went through the Spiritual Exercises. Though the chaplaincy of her new Institute was transferred to the Franciscans, Jesuits continued their close association with her. Fr Lee advised her closely in drafting a petition for recognition to Pope Paul V in 1615. On his death, his nephew, Fr Henry Lee continued to advise her for many years."

However, in this chosen apostolate of the education of girls, much was added to the Jesuit curriculum which had the Spiritual Exercises as its centre. " In the classes (we) will teach a sense of duty, Christian doctrine, good morals, reading the common and Latin languages, writing, household management . . . singing , painting, sewing, spinning, curtain making, in a word, all those liberal exercises which are more suitable for every state of life." This is quite an impressive curriculum by any reckoning. What is particularly interesting is the emphasis Mary Ward put on modern languages; all her life she urged her companions to become fluent in the language where they were living, and regretted her limitations in German.

Though she and her companions had to live mostly abroad, she never deviated from her first and enduring desire to serve the Catholic families of England, "to do something for England". I do not think that she ever thought that the work of her Institute should only be concerned with the running of schools—that in itself would have been a constraint—but, given the discussions and indeed tensions in the present IBVM about how best to use their lives, it is important to remind people that she wanted to teach, and to teach girls; and that her followers founded schools. However little time she spent in schools, I see her as one of the the first great teachers of girls. This task could be achieved only if she and her companions could be given a Rule that provided them with the same freedom as men enjoyed.

In the years after her death, the small band of her companions had to accept, as I have shewn already, the fiction of beginning a new Institute, in which they would have outwardly to conform, live a form of enclosed life, and wear a religious habit. The degree of enclosure has varied over time and place. Even Mother Cecilia Marshall, at Ascot in the 1900s, on the one hand could encourage her Sisters to swim in the school's pool, ride bicycles around the countryside, and travel unaccompanied, even drive motor cars, while on the other hand, they had to live conventually, and wear a notably religious habit. Many of the continental houses became indistinguishable in their observance of religious routines and devotions from other female orders, and many are markedly conservative to this day.

On Mary Ward's death, Barbara Babthorpe, who was in Rome at the time, took over what few there remained of her companions. They were scattered, and their number is not known. Sister M. Pia, the present Provincial in England, says that there were perhaps no more than fifteen; how many in England is certainly not known, not least because of the fear of the consequences of admitting it. For example, a Sister Dorothea lived and worked from Hindlesham House in Essex, but never declared herself a member of the Institute. When Barbara Babthorpe died, she was succeeded by Mary Poyntz, who moved to Augsburg in the Imperial territories. Augsburg became effectively the central point in the life of the Institute.

Under the hazardous protection of Charles II's wife, Catherine of Braganza, Frances Bedingfield opened a house and school in Hammersmith in 1669, which survived even the horror of the Titus Oates Plot in 1678. In the brief respite from persecution and oppression of English Catholics that came with the accession of James II in 1685, Frances Bedingfield (who had first joined Mary Ward at the age of fourteen and taken her vows in Santa Maria Maggiore in Rome) was able to return from Augsburg, to which she had fled for shelter, to establish a convent and school in York in 1686. The Papal recognition of 1703, conditional on banning any mention of Mary Ward, compelled the Sisters to take her memory underground. The Bull *Quamvis Justo* of Benedict XIV in 1749 drove this point home, and they had to endure such comments on the Painted Life as those made by officials of the Curia of the Bishop of Augsburg—"More than thirty paintings portraying visions, revelations, ecstasies and apparitions, all unfounded, displayed for all to see. They should be completely banished." The Painted Life was taken down, the pictures removed from their frames, rolled up and stored away; letters and documents were not destroyed but Mary Ward's signatures were cut off. There were some bonfires. The only trace that remained was the labelling of these Sisters as "Englischen Fraulein", made respectable by recording on their gravestones that they were all "high-born".

The prominence of Augsburg led me rather to think that, in effect, it was by default the founding house, but Sister Gillian Orchard has corrected me by pointing out that in 1621 Christopher Paradeiser bequeathed his Schloss Nymphenburg in Munich to the Elector of Bavaria, who handed it over to the infant Institute some time around 1626. The Sisters remained in this house until it was closed by the secularisation policy of Napoleon in 1808; they refounded the house in 1835 in another part of the city. She also reminded me that other early foundations, for example in Rome itself, antedate Augsburg. Sister Gillian also told me that "successive Mothers General—Mary Ward, Barbara Babthorpe, Mary Poyntz, etc.—always resided in Rome when not on their travels", until 1703, when residence in Munich or Augsburg became the common practice. It may be that I have a particular interest in Mary Poyntz, which I cannot explain, and it is true that from her foundation in Augsburg in 1662, this house has been very important to the English IBVM; Ascot is the daughter of Augsburg. It was unavoidable that the Sisters were dependent on princely patronage and episcopal supervision, so that Mary Ward's urgent desire for freedom of movement and obedience only to Rome could not be realised. The schools that they established were far more for the daughters of the wealthy and the well-to-do than for ordinary girls, though wherever possible , they ran parallel schools for poor girls.

The isolation of Britain from continental Europe in the French Revolutionary and Napoleonic periods, an isolation that seems to have continued for some years after 1815, left the Bar Convent severed from the rest of the IBVM. Founded from Augsburg in York in 1686, the Sisters there felt so cut off and lacking in guidance that in 1809 they asked for the supervision and protection of the Vicar Apostolic of the Northern District, and they took a Dominican Father as their chaplain. This step, seen as so necessary by a lonely community, nevertheless was felt by continental houses to be such an act of betrayal that its return to the mainstream of what was by then an essentially German-Austrian Institute, was achieved with some difficulty. This Teutonic dominance was accepted, though reluctantly, by Mother Cecilia Marshall, and it was generally pleasing that the year, 1929, that saw the creation of an English Province (284 years after Mary Ward's death), saw also the transference of the centre of the Institute back to Rome.

The Bar Convent was the greatest single achievement of the IBVM continuously from 1686. The work of the Sisters, at first more for the daughters of the well-to-do gentry—wives often kept the Faith when husbands lapsed—but also for the middling and poor folk, full of difficulties in the first half of the nineteenth century, slowly came to be appreciated greatly in the city and the surrounding countryside. Many of the Sisters were formidably proficient in languages. Frances Bedingfield knew Hebrew, Latin and Greek; French, Italian and German were certainly taught in the school. To teach German in those years was a phenomenon. The Sisters also took over the Jesuit emphasis on play-acting as a means of developing good speaking and self-confidence. The school at Ascot was a very modest affair in comparison, until recent years.

The Bar Convent's exterior presented blank brick walls to the world, but inside, on the first floor, there was the most beautiful chapel, used by the faithful many years before Catholic public worship became normal. It has survived a very uneven history, including the bombing and the death of five Sisters in 1942, to teach many generations of girls from the district and a much wider world. Eventually in 1985 it joined with two other Catholic schools to form a mixed comprehensive school. The building itself became a museum of Northern Catholic life; it is now entering an even more extraordinary era as an outpost of the new de Montfort University of Leicester.

It was to York that the Archbishop of Dublin sent a young woman, Frances Ball, to be apprenticed, so-to-speak, into the Institute. Formally professed, she returned to Dublin in 1822 as Mother Teresa to establish a school in Rathfarnham. She took great care to use constitutions that were the closest she could get to Mary Ward's own intentions. She had them printed in Dublin in 1832, to be used wherever new Houses were founded. From Mother Teresa's determination to live in the spirit of the Holy Family, all her houses were named after Loreto, the place in Italy to which in legend the home of the Holy Family had been miraculously transported. Her work expanded to cover the world, always concentrating on teaching and on an unwavering desire to follow the Jesuit model. In effect, this major expansion came to form an independent Generalate. In 1928, a young Albanian woman joined the Dublin House. She is now universally known as Mother Teresa of Calcutta. She has written of "my deep gratitude to the Loreto branch of the Institute for the twenty years I spent with the Sisters . . . In gratitude to Mary Ward I pray that her daughters . . . may continue to be a sign of the Church today, by reflecting the motherhood of Mary in forming other 'Marys' to carry Jesus to all those they meet."

In the September of 1847, Mother Teresa Ball responded to a request from the Bishop of Toronto to send Sisters to teach the Catholic children of his diocese. From appallingly difficult beginnings, the work flourished, so that today this part of the IBVM, which they spell as Loretto, has thirty houses in Canada and the United States, and forms a third Generalate.

Only in 1953 did the three branches or Generalates of the IBVM agree to work closely, but still separately, each with its headquarters in Rome. The branch with which we are concerned is the Roman, and the Irish and the Canadian branches continue in their own right. Mother Cecilia Marshall seems to have viewed them guardedly, for though Mother Teresa Ball was convinced that she had adhered to Mary Ward's original intentions most faithfully, Mother Cecilia felt differently. Regretfully admitting that the Roman Branch was so German dominated, she still acknowledged it as the trunk rather than as a branch. "I quite agree that the German element is very strong . . . the Bavarians are the stem of the Institute and not a branch." Writing later in a series of letters to Mother M. Campion Davenport, she observed that "I must tell you that I was not elected General in 1929 as I made it clear that I could not accept the government of an Institute that was so largely made up of German-speaking members, and so I did not receive a majority of votes and had not to refuse." In 1929 the three Generalates had at any rate agreed to establish their own regional provincialates. The English Province is part of the Roman Generalate, deriving from Mary Poyntz in Augsburg. Cecilia Marshall was the first Provincial.

In common with almost all religious orders until recently, the IBVM distinguished between the teaching and the household Sisters. Once they had settled into conventual patterns, quite contrary to Mary Ward's purposes but more or less inevitably under the historical circumstances, this was shown in a distinction between "choir" and "lay", between teachers and ancillaries. They had separate novitiates , very different in nature and quality, and somewhat different dress. These distinctions are now looked back on by many Sisters with embarrassment; the lay Sisters were loyal backstairs servants, on whose labours generations depended. The newest "choir novice" took precedence over them. Herein lay the use of the terms "Mother" and "Sister", until the general reform in the 1970s. The lists of Superiors and Headmistresses in Appendix 6 illustrates the point nicely, as does a visit to the burial ground at Ascot. Mother Cecilia's grave has a taller cross than the rest. May one, naughtily, suggest that it illustrates a third layer, occupied in splendid isolation by Mother Cecilia? Photographs will show how the dress of the IBVM in the English Province —not by any means universally—has moved from the full habit of most people's memory, by stages, through to the secular dress of today; in other words, back to what the foundress so desired. Some of the older Sisters still prefer a modified form of the habit.

Since Vatican II, the Institute has moved towards a full freedom to use the Ignatian Exercises. In 1978, it was allowed finally to take the Jesuit Constitutions, but even then "only in so far as they are applicable to women". As Sister Gillian Orchard said in the centenary edition of the school magazine in 1985: "Do I hear the Foundress groan in her grave, wherever it may be?" The pressure to conform and to be like other women's religious orders had perhaps been heavier in the years after the First Vatican Council in 1870 than at any previous time. It may be that the greatest achievement of Mother Cecilia Marshall, more than even the development of the school at Ascot, was her successful fight to preserve what she saw as the essentials of Mary Ward's purposes: no enclosure, no Office in Choir, no episcopal control, women to be governed by women. Writing in the years 1949 to 1952 to her friend Mother M. Campion, who was at that time Assistant to the Mother General in Rome, she said "I am so delighted that you are standing up for our dear Foundress, and shewing them that she wanted to be a Jesuit in every way."

The Institute is now untrammelled, and free to develop fully in the spirit of Mary Ward. A Provincial Congregation met at Ascot in 1992, and there has been a General Congregation of the whole body at Ascot in July 1993 (see Appendix 2). The obverse of this freedom and independence is that it takes away all the obvious props and supports of the conventual life and may bring a very noticeable loneliness to individual Sisters. Each Sister is very much on her own in her essential religious life, except that she is encouraged to have a spiritual director, an entirely private matter; through this person her life is scrutinised and developed. This is what Mary Ward wanted: no detailed order of the day, no "Opus Dei" in the Benedictine sense. The Institute pursues Ignatian and not Benedictine spirituality, with no immutable routines, and no protective safety from the world. Here is Mother Cecilia, writing again to Mother Campion: "I must say I feel very warm to Fr Grisar when I hear that he adores Mary Ward and wants the Institute to keep her idea of it. We are certainly going away from it by adopting these Benedictine rites etc." Or again:

> I should never think we needed white dresses to make us realise the purity of religious life. If we rely on these things we shall certainly not have the solid virtue that Mary Ward said should be highly prized . . . If we are going to found our Institute on people who are only attracted by such things, I pity it . . . I don't feel that we need have a Manual at all, the Jesuits certainly have none. It ties one down too much to particular devotions . . . I was sorry to hear that Fr Zeiger has the wrong idea of our Institute. Perhaps he thinks that 'we are but women' and so must have these externals to attract us to God. If so he has completely misinterpreted our beloved Mary Ward's spirit . . . Rites and Ceremonies are good and beautiful and helpful in other Orders, but they are not for us, because our Foundress wants us to be like the Jesuits who have none of these things.

The wisdom of Mother Cecilia is most refreshing to read, and there is much more of it in a private compilation made by Sister Mark. Perhaps an epitome of her views lies in this passage: "As we don't have ceremonies for Clothing, there's no question of white dresses and I hope there never will be. I asked Fr Corbishley whether the Jesuits had any ceremony when getting their gown, and he said it was just thrown on their beds the night before."

So the Sisters mostly live in community houses, some quite small, and the Institute has to have the resources to look after, to nurse, and to provide medical care for its sick and aged members. For the younger ones, only a cross on a chain and wedding ring to Christ mark them out at all, and as this can be also the "gear" of the unconventional and the drop-out, it is not particularly noticeable.

What may strike the outsider sharply is the starkness of the IBVM pattern of life.

In recent years, many Sisters have negotiated varied new forms of Apostolic work. There is a decline in the desire to teach, especially in independent schools which are by definition for the children of the well-to-do. This is a contentious issue. One is left to muse and ponder over whether the retreat from one of Mary Ward's chief intentions, which was to teach Catholic girls, is depriving the IBVM of one of its clearest historical identities. Mary wrote on another occasion that "Besides attending to our own perfection, we desire to devote ourselves with all diligence and prudent zeal to promote or procure the salvation of our neighbour by the education of girls, or by any other means that are congruous to the times." This does modify the idea of singleness of purpose, and so may justify the pursuit of other forms of apostolate by the Sisters, especially in recent years.

Religious Orders have never established schools simply to be ordinary schools. Undoubtedly, one purpose, implicit if not explicit, has been to draw new members from their pupils. It has to be acknowledged that many Orders have a considerable history of indoctrination, or of attempts to indoctrinate. Some of the male Orders have given the impression that they thought that pupils could be beaten into shape, and, in many girls' convent schools, rules of extraordinary detail, even pettiness, have often prevailed. It must be said that the IBVM has no such history. Mary Ward not only drew up a remarkable and broad curriculum, but also held strong views about the need for gentle ways in discipline: "when teaching the Sisters shall try to ensure that erring or delinquent pupils be punished solely by the awareness of admitted and acknowledged error and shame. Thus it will come about that they will be ashamed to transgress." Mother Cecilia Marshall built her Ascot on gentleness and civilised manners. It was to be a school for young ladies. This, in her time, did bring a sense of who was acceptable and who was not, but it was never obtrusive. It was held to be unfair to bring in girls who would not fit. The aim was to build a strong and warm sense of family, wrapped in Catholic piety and practice, perhaps cosy and inward-looking at times. This has produced the outstanding affection and loyalty seen in succeeding generations of Old Girls, which has shewn itself so clearly in the astonishingly generous response to the various Appeals.

As I have noted already, I cannot find that there has been, or is, one simple pocket rule book for the Institute. There are some abbreviated versions from different years in the archive at the Bar Convent. What is now required is a sixth months' postulancy, followed by a two years' novitiate. First vows then lead to final profession, over a minimum period of six years; the whole formation takes eight years. This Jesuit model omits, obviously, their own years of priestly training (which takes them up to sixteen years). Simple vows are renewed twice a year. What is minimally required of an IBVM Sister in any twenty-four hours is half an hour of private prayer (there is no obligation to say the Office), and an examination of conscience; attendance at Mass is desirable but not compulsory. Sister Pia, the English Provincial, has told me that "examination of conscience" should be much more than stock-taking of the day; rather, a severe review of the state of one's life, "an examination of consciousness". Each Sister is required to live through the Ignatian Exercises once a year. I asked Sister Mark to give her answers to two questions:

1. What is the essence of Ignatian spirituality?
2. What is an IBVM vocation?

She replied that the essence must be the Spiritual Exercises. It is they that give the impetus to seek "the greater good", to discern what God is calling one to be and to do, and to be a disciple of Christ always ministering to those in need. The full Spiritual Exercises, which take thirty days, are made twice in the lifetime of a Jesuit or an IBVM Sister. The eight-day annual Retreat is a participation in the Exercises. The Examen of Consciousness which is done twice daily is to ensure that one is walking as closely as possible in the spirit of the Lord.

Writing about vocations to the IBVM , she describes them as

a call by God to follow the charism of Mary Ward who based her
congregation on that of the Society of Jesus. She wanted the
Ignatian Constitutions to be the foundation document of her
Sisters. Even now Rome does not allow the Institute to have the
full constitutions though there are hopes to have them soon.
IBVM Novices and Juniors should therefore follow the same pattern of formation as the Jesuits do. The aim is to produce spiritu-
ally and intellectually mature men and women who are free to
follow Christ under obedience. The IBVM that I grew up with
did not have the Spiritual Exercises in their fullness as we do
today. The thirty days retreat was only just coming in and was
preached at us as a group rather than directed on a one-to-one
basis. Spiritual direction, which is essential in Ignatian Spirituality, was non-existent. Instead, we studied large books which
were much more monastic in tone. The life and routine of Novices was likewise monastic in style, with fixed hours for prayer,
labour, and recreation, all of us together. We took this for
granted, and yet deplored the monastic practices of other congregations who were more monastic than us. At least the IBVM
were able to aspire to higher education and to travel alone. The
fact that we were less monastic than others was due to Mother
Cecilia Marshall, but this led to a certain complacency which
meant that when the changes from Vatican II came along, the
IBVM did not believe or realise that there was much to be
learned.

In recent times, Mary Ward's determination to have freedom of
movement has been fully recovered and it is clear that the English
IBVM pioneered this, whereas many of the continental houses have
kept more of the conventual life. It is most interesting to become
aware of the tension through the centuries between the Foundress's
determination to be Jesuit, and the social pressures that obliged the
Sisters to accept a greater or lesser degree of conventual life with its

easily followed unvarying routines. The preoccupation, certainly in the English Province, is with the over-riding importance of being available for any and every requirement of the Apostolate.

Sister Mark, in her own life, illustrates much of what has just been written. She was a pupil in the school from 1955 to 1961 (taking A Levels in one year as was the practice in the school at that time); a postulant in 1962, a novice in 1963; she took first vows in 1965, and was professed finally in 1971. She also illustrates a further development, again very much the achievement of Mother Cecilia who had insisted that Sisters should be free to travel on their own and to enter higher education; she was a university student from 1965 to 1968, taking her post-graduate certificate in Education in 1969—fitting these intensive studies into the years from first vows to final profession. She has told me that she was taught by or under the influence of the IBVM from the age of three. It was only when she became a postulant in 1962 that she was taught anything of significance about St Ignatius, and until the great liberation of the 1970s the Institute, and indeed the Society of Jesus itself had, over the long years, settled into an incomplete and over-formalised practice of the Spiritual Exercises. Even those Retreats, of which there is so much mention in the records of the Institute, and in the school magazine, had become passive episodes of silence broken by spiritual lectures.

She returned to Ascot to teach History and Religious Education, and to be librarian, from 1969 to 1981. An all-too-brief time in the IBVM school in Cambridge gave her an opportunity to experience some of the life of the city and of the university. There she had a sort of premonition that she would be brought back quite soon to be headmistress. So she was, when Sister Emmanuel became seriously ill. By any reckoning, she was thrown in at the deep end. The educational world had changed greatly from the time when people were appointed to headships without any real form of phased preparatory training, and yet she was put in to face a school in need of a great deal of re-thinking, not only about management but about the whole curriculum itself. The last ten years are the measure of her achievement.

Sister Mark exemplifies what Pope John Paul II had in mind when, during his pastoral visit to Britain in May and June 1982, he made two references to Mary Ward. Meeting four thousand men and women Religious at Digby Stuart College in Roehampton, he talked about "that extraordinary Yorkshire woman, Mary Ward, who became a pioneer of the active unenclosed congregations for women". Ascot, and the other IBVM schools are now run by "active unenclosed" women. The Pope continued to single out the Foundress later on in his visit; on the Knavesmire at York, on the feast of the Visitation of The Blessed Virgin Mary, he said,

> I am conscious of the history, especially the religious history, of this part of England. I refer to Holy Island where Aidan and Cuthbert brought the Catholic faith. I recall Bede, who wrote so lovingly of the early life of the Church in England. I remember that a thousand years later, men and women laid down their lives here for the faith they loved. Mary Ward taught the Gospel of Jesus Christ . . . Margaret Clitherow gave her life in this city of York. These holy women inspire women today to take their rightful place in the life of the Church, as befits their equality of rights and particular dignity.

Margaret Clitherow has been canonised, and in the course of studying the life and influence of Mary Ward, I have become increasingly aware of the amount of work that has been put into the promotion of her Cause too, work which after so much energy and dedication right through to the 1950s, seems to be less in evidence at present. Pope John Paul's words were a handsome reversal of the deplorable attitudes of some of his predecessors, but even though Pius XII referred to her as "that incomparable woman", I remain puzzled about the official attitude of the Church to Mary Ward. I have no knowledge that the charges laid against her, including that of heresy, have ever been withdrawn. It is in the nature of the Papacy that one major statement cannot openly be contradicted by another, so that ways round problems have to be found. The tortuous path, bringing Mary Ward from condemnation to canonisation, is not yet completed, but at long last, after the Second Vatican Council, the Institute can rejoice openly and freely in honouring its Foundress.

The English contribution to the institutional and devotional life of the Church is immeasurable, but in all the Church's history, there have been only two English founders of religious Orders or Congregations. Dom David Knowles, in his works on the monastic Orders in medieval England, pays proper respect to St Gilbert of Sempringham (died 1189), who established nunneries to which groups of men, often priests, were attached, creating double houses of men and women, each with its own cloister and accommodation; they met together in church. At its height, there were 1500 nuns, and altogether 2200 Gilbertines. This entirely English Order, confirmed by Eugenius III in 1148, never ventured beyond England. Nothing whatsoever survived the Dissolution. Dom David also pointed out that, after the Conquest, no woman Religious in community achieved anything noteworthy in the spiritual or academic life. Mary Ward, born into recusancy and persecution, established a Congregation that, at first entirely Western European (substantially German and Austrian), now stretches across the world. The election, in the recent General Chapter in July 1993, of a South Korean Sister as the Head of the whole Roman Branch may be a pointer to altogether new developments.

2

The Recusant World:
Catholic Life in England, 1560 to 1850

The Act Against Recusants of 1593, by using the label in a state document, brought the recusants onto the public stage as an identifiable group of people. They were the ones who refused (*recusare*) to acknowledge the Elizabethan Church Settlement; they rejected it. Others, still hopeful that they might swing things their way, were called dissenters (in this same year there was an Act against Puritans). That the recusants were recognised as being in a different category was indicated by the virulence of the language used about them—"sundry wicked and seditious persons, who, terming themselves Catholics, and being indeed spies and intelligencers . . . rebellious and traitorous subjects . . . hiding their most detestable and devilish purposes under a false pretext of religion and conscience, do secretly wander and shift from place to place . . . to corrupt and seduce Her Majesty's subjects." The Act required that everyone above the age of sixteen should attend the Anglican parish church, that if disobedient they should be forbidden to travel further than five miles from their home, and gave the precise wording of an act of submission to be made publicly in church, the incumbent of which was made responsible for compliance. So began policies of ever-increasing ferocity against those who acknowledged the papal supremacy.

Mary Ward was seven years old when the Act Against Recusants was passed. A journey into "Mary Ward Country" would be unprofitable now. "The names of Mulwith, Newby and Givendale still survive in the neighbourhood of Ripon. Givendale and Mulwith are only farm houses of a far more modern date. Newby Hall (which also belonged to her father) is a handsome building of Queen Anne's reign." So wrote Catherine Chambers in 1882. The house at Mulwith in which she was born and brought up was burnt down and the family moved. When she was five, she went to live with her grandmother, the formidable Mrs Wright, who "with her husband was then leading a very holy life in great seclusion, after having endured severe persecutions for the Faith". Mrs Wright had spent many years in gaol, had organised worship and prayer with fellow prisoners, and outfaced her accusers, notably the Earl of Huntingdon, President of the Council of the North from 1572 to 1599. Her sons, John and Christopher, Mary's uncles, were to be two of the chief conspirators in the Gunpowder Plot, in which they lost their lives. Mary Ward stayed with her grandmother for five years. In 1597–8, when persecution was fierce, she went to live with a relation, Mrs Ardington of Harewell near Pateley Bridge in the Yorkshire Dales; later on she lived at Babthorpe, ten miles to the south of York. After a life of travels and tribulations she died in Heworth in 1645, then a separate village from York, and was buried in the parish churchyard at Osbaldwick, a further one and a half miles from York, "by a minister who was honest enough to be bribed", as Mary Poyntz put it in *A Briefe Relation* . . .

This is thin material for a biographer, with little for the walker to see. All that matters is that there were recusant households in the York–Ripon area; the further one went into the sparsely populated moorland, the more recusancy could be found. Inland from Whitby, to this day, there are "recusant" parishes at Ugthorpe, Egton Bridge and Leaholme. Whitby was an easy place of entry and exit, a flourishing port remarkably remote from the populous areas of Yorkshire. Catherine Chambers makes the interesting point that, by the 1590s, Catholic gentlemen saw it wise to live as obscurely as possible, even to the point of keeping their genealogy quiet; one can only sketch out Mary Ward's family history, but her parents and grandparents—given the notion of twenty-five years as a generation—had grown up in the world of Henry VIII, Edward VI and Mary.

Until the national curriculum laid out the specific areas of study in history for the ages seven, eleven and fourteen, in chronological order from the ancient, through the medieval to the modern world, the commonest practice in schools was to study English history from 1485. The medieval was usually a perfunctory preface, and in next to no time pupils were dealing with "the Reformation" (before which, England was "Roman Catholic"). The religious changes from 1530 onwards were explained as justified by the decline in real acceptance of the "old Faith", a proliferation of superficialities, and increasing corruption and immorality in the clergy and religious. A sense of inevitable progression towards the Elizabethan Settlement was conveyed. Just as Herbert Butterfield attacked the "Whig Interpretation of History", seen as an irresistible progress towards constitutional monarchy, so there has been a "Protestant Interpretation of History", imbibed by almost all the population. There has been very little "come-back" to all this from Catholic writers until recently; John Lingard (1771 – 1851: his *History of England* was written between 1819 and 1830) was the first great pioneer—a contemporary of Macaulay, but not nearly so readable or influential. Now, in Eamon Duffy's *The Stripping of the Altars* (1992), there is a scholarly and reasonable revision and re-interpretation of the years 1400 to 1580.

Catholicism was not moribund, religious life had not slackened, the general population, with a thousand years of practice behind it, was woven into the liturgy. Church authorities certainly did not wish or permit vernacular versions of the Bible; the Latin of the Vulgate was seen as timeless and totally reliable. It was authentic, and it was thought that popular translations would carry dangers. But, printing had been normal since the 1470s, and there was no lack of supplementary guides to the Mass to help the populace. The greater number of days in the year was dedicated to Feast Days and Saints, some of which carried the most detailed liturgical observance; in the later medieval Church, Corpus Christi, a summer festival, was immensely important and popular. In their Wills, people of substance indicated a clear understanding and acceptance of

Church doctrine especially that of Purgatory. Church decoration of every kind reflected a general understanding of Catholic teaching. It is too simple to think that there was a society in which the more educated understood, and the less educated lived in idolatrous superstition. Not only were there the parish churches—and where the great Benedictine abbeys stood near towns, their naves—there were also guild churches, house churches at the ends of streets, and many chantry chapels. Large private houses had their own chapels. There were thought to be seventy-nine chapels and churches, large and small, in fourteenth-century Winchester, with a population of about three and a half thousand. Particularly through dramatic presentations, processions, ceremonies and rituals with appropriate clothing, the many high points of the liturgical year were a living part of everyone's life. They were taught in many more ways than through homilies and official public sermons; statuary, glass and painting amply illustrated familiarity with the Bible and the liturgy.

The Reformation was carried through by a series of Acts of State. England and Wales, with entirely sea borders (except for the one with Scotland, which was independent) were easily governable countries provided central authority was efficient. When one deals with Royal Commissioners fanning out into every part of the kingdom, they were not venturing into unknown territories. We are familiar, in our own time, with the imposition of power by minorities, provided they have been willing to be completely ruthless. The governments of Henry VIII, Edward VI, Mary and Elizabeth were all single-minded in the exercise of power. Their purposes differed, but none could countenance the idea of permitted dissent. "Cuius Regio, eius religio." Modern tolerance has come much more from indifferentism than from passionate conviction.

Like many another, I have turned over in my mind, in the light of what is accurately known about the richness of religious life until the 1530s, why events unfolded as they did between 1535 and 1570. At first, only one bishop, John Fisher, a saintly man but whose See of Rochester was perhaps the least important, resisted Henry VIII to the point of death; only one outstanding layman, Thomas More, did likewise. Most of the abbots, priors and abbesses went quietly to their pensions or to new jobs under the new dispensation; the Carthusians of the London Charterhouse were heroes and saints, but that is not the general picture in the country. Abbeys were stripped of everything portable and sellable, and their shells became easy quarries for generations to come. It is not possible to believe that all the bishops facing Henry VIII were closet Protestants, like Cranmer, who had been biding their time. The greater number of bishops had been, for many centuries, promoted from the Royal service; some others, often foreign, were direct Papal nominees. They were at home in administration, and were at ease when summoned to Parliaments. So were the "Mitred Abbots", that is, the heads of the greater Houses. The laity, in uprisings up and down the country, and particularly in the Pilgrimage of Grace of 1536, came nearer than ever the bishops did, to stopping the King in his tracks. They dispersed because they believed the Royal promises to stay loyal to the Faith, and went home to be picked off singly or in small groups, arrested and killed.

It is important to remember that "Ecclesia Anglicana" was simply two provinces of the Universal Church; Scotland was separate and indeed seen as missionary territory, and the various efforts to create a third Province, whether for the Midlands or for Wales, had failed. It is easy to find out the biographical details concerning bishops, but extremely difficult to be sure of the training, even of the quality of ordination of ordinary clergy—a matter taken up in the Councils of Trent (1545 – 63) with the requirement for the establishment of metropolitan or diocesan seminaries. It was the pre-Tridentine clergy who faced the fury of Reformation; by Mary Ward's time, the priests on the English Mission were either Jesuit or seminary-trained, and often the stuff of martyrdom.

The Act in Restraint of Appeals to Rome of 1533 is rightly seen as the decisive affirmation of a separate English State, possessed of full sovereignty, than which there was nothing higher. The lawyers deftly mistranslated "Ecclesia Anglicana" as "The Church of England", so opening the door to the notion of the "branch theory", namely that the Universal Church consists of three equally valid branches growing out of something called the "Early Church": the Latin, the Orthodox, and the English (splendidly illustrated in a Victorian wall-painting in the parish church of Helmsley in north Yorkshire).

The Henrician bishops made the immense mistake of misreading the situation, of not realising Cranmer's ultimate purposes, and of not grasping that, once the monastic lands had been distributed and sold, an unshifting vested interest in the new state of affairs had been created. Not even Mary persisted in trying to undo this, and Elizabeth consolidated it.

The "Protestant Interpretation of History" sees the reign of Mary as a regrettable interlude but a useful reminder of what might have happened if the papists had truly regained power. Mercifully, it lasted only five years. (In this century, Lenin, believing in the inevitability of history, allowed that the process might be slowed down for a while by awkward people, but that nothing could stop it.) Eamon Duffy not only speculates on what the course of history might have been if Mary had reigned for thirty or forty years, but also produces ample evidence that clergy and laity alike, in the later years of Henry, and in the time of Edward's Protectors, hid away vestments and other portables, not obeying the orders of the Commissioners. They were unable to prevent the destruction of rood screens, glass, statuary and stonework—though even here, Duffy's photographs shew how much was missed. When Mary acceded, to general relief and rejoicing, the hidden treasures were brought out and the old liturgy resumed.

Mary's half-sister Elizabeth had learnt from experience to keep her opinions to herself, and she acquiesced not very willingly or gracefully in a Catholic coronation service; it proved extremely difficult to find a bishop to crown her, but Bishop Oglethorpe of Carlisle was prevailed upon to do so (Canterbury was vacant from the death of Cardinal Pole, Heath of York and Tunstall of Durham refused). But, pointedly, she withdrew at the Communion, and within a year had ensured that her first Parliament enacted the Acts of Uniformity and Settlement, the rocks on which the Established Church is built, with the Thirty-Nine Articles of 1563 as a definite body of doctrine. The Act of Uniformity was carried by a majority of three in the Lords, without the support of a single bishop. All the bishops present were deprived of their Sees. The last bishop of the ancient hierarchy, Bishop Goldwell, died in Rome in 1585; there was no-one left with sufficient authority to regulate and coordinate the lives of English Catholics. From 1598 until 1685, a variety of inadequate arrangements was made, leaving secular clergy and monks usually at loggerheads. The ordinary clergy, no doubt weary and bemused by decades of change, sometimes accepted, sometimes did not; they, more than the bishops, seem to have thought that the storms would pass, and matters return to whatever was "normal". We do not know as much as we should about the clergy from 1560 to 1570. In that year came the Bull, *Regnans in Excelsis*, declaring Elizabeth a heretic and her subjects "to be absolved for ever from all fidelity and obedience", so placing people in the most appalling quandary. In 1555 Pope Paul IV had ruled that holy orders administered under the Edwardine Rites were null and void. Leo XIII repeated the ruling in 1896.

Pressure, sometimes intermittent, but always there, fell on the laity, to attend the parish church weekly or be fined, to face an increase in fines for persistent refusal. The policy of hitting through the pocket and property, twelve pence for each act of non-attendance, was seen to have more potential than imprisonment in a society that had no regular prison system. In 1577, letters were sent to all the bishops requiring them to complete a schedule of the papists within their jurisdiction. (This practice was to continue for two hundred years and more, listing the papists wherever they were to be found.) In 1581 a fine of twenty pounds a month was imposed on persistent refusers, a crippling figure. All evidence suggests that, at this time, and for many years to come, such a policy was applied sometimes severely, sometimes selectively, sometimes weakly. Many Catholics lived more or less in peace with their neighbours, especially in rural areas, but always with the possibility that things could turn sour at very short notice. When one adds to this the obstacles posed when inheriting property, getting married or buried, a picture emerges of recusant life lived in tension with the likelihood of tragedy ever present.

Women as well as men were caught in these difficulties, and John Bossy has made the point forcefully that mothers and grandmothers were imprisoned, but also were, in so many cases, the guardians of instruction and practice for their children, the centres of strength and stability. He underlines this in the example of Mary Ward, who grew up in a matriarchal society—and therefore had no difficulty in advancing the case for the importance of women in the Church. He also reflects that because these circumstances were not found on the Continent, and certainly not in Italy, her proposals for an Institute for women based on the Jesuit Constitutions were viewed with alarm and shock by cardinals in Rome.

By the 1570s, it had to be faced that a new order was slowly settling in; there was no point in hiding vestments or altar tables in the belief that the old order would return. The medieval church had ended, and new ways would have to be found to train priests, and to keep the old Faith alive. This could not take place in England. William Allen brought together a small group of young men at Douai in 1568 to provide "a perpetual feed and supply of Catholics, namely of the clergy". Bossy also indicates how modest and tentative Allen's thinking was, still based on a belief that the Elizabethan Settlement would collapse, and that all that was needed was a sort of institution-in-waiting. As a former Oxford don himself, he seems to have wanted to establish a temporary place of refuge for the considerable number of other dons who left England; over 100 left Oxford during the first ten years of Elizabeth's reign, 27 from New College alone. Allen was, it would seem, soon pushed into more activity and into a completely new role; the Protestant Settlement was not going to pass quickly, priests would have to be trained, in substantial numbers, and sent back to the English Mission, to face likely arrest and death because the Elizabethan government had turned nasty in the Act Against Jesuits and

Seminarists of 1585, followed by the Act Against Recusants of 1593.

Those who wished to follow the religious life, men and women, had to go to the Continent. By 1607, only one monk of the pre-Reformation Benedictine Congregation of Westminster survived. On the 21st November of that year, Dom Sigebert Buckley was given Papal permission to aggregate two English monks of the Cassinese Congregation to his own, thus ensuring a certain continuity of the English Congregation with St Dunstan, St Wilfrid and St Augustine. The new House was called St Gregory's at Douai in Flanders; another centre of English monastic life began at St Laurence's, at Dieulouard in Lorraine.

Houses for women proliferated in Flanders and France; one that might be singled out is that established at Cambrai by the great-great-granddaughter of St Thomas More—Helen, who took the veil as Dame Gertrude; this was to become the notable Abbey of Stanbrook in 1838. In 1612, a nun who had been a companion of St Teresa of Avila established a Carmelite convent in Antwerp. One of its first nuns was Anne Worsley, who became the first-ever English Carmelite nun—there had been no Carmelite nunnery in pre-Reformation England. In 1619 she became the first Prioress of an English Carmel. Margaret Clitherow, who, with her unborn child had been pressed to death in York in 1586, had another daughter Anne, who became an Augustinian Canoness at Louvain in 1598. Such people and many others, had to be supported largely by their families in England, and often lived in considerable poverty.

The great exception was Mary Ward. What she founded was a Company, a Congregation, an Institute, a Society, but not an enclosed Community. It was not until the eighteenth century that, quietly and discreetly, a handful of schools for boys could be set up in England, but Mary Ward's followers had already founded the school in Hammersmith in 1669, and the Bar Convent in York. Through all its vicissitudes the Bar Convent never closed, whereas the House and school in Hammersmith had a more chequered history, and faded out in 1795.

After the Restoration of Charles II in 1660, the laws against

Catholics were tightened. There was a near impossibility of inheriting property (this was a threat that could be held "in terroram", not
always applied—or else there would have been no landed recusant
families) and recurrent fining. They were excluded from all public
office and from the universities. In the Titus Oates episode they
were most ferociously persecuted, an act that was tolerated by that
weary cynic the king who was converted to Catholicism on his
death-bed. There is the unquantifiable matter of what protection
was afforded to some Catholics from the fact that both Charles I
and Charles II had Catholic wives. There is some evidence that
Mary Ward's last return to England and her final residence in
Heworth was possible because she and her small group were not
actively hindered. When Royalist York fell to the Parliamentarians
after the battle of Marston Moor, her last year was much grimmer.
As already mentioned, the establishment of the Hammersmith
Convent and school was made possible by the influence of Charles
II's wife. This was slender enough, and the Sisters lived dangerously
during the Titus Oates outrage of 1678, but they survived.

Suddenly, in 1685, came the prospect of relief; the new king, James
II, was openly Catholic. Priests and Religious were publicly present
at Court, and the Pope was able to make some episcopal provision
for English Catholics for the first time since 1558, by creating the
four Districts, London, Midland, Western and Northern, with a
Vicar Apostolic over each, separately and publicly consecrated in
the Chapel Royal in London. The system of Vicars Apostolic was to
last until 1850; in 1840, the four Districts became eight, and in 1850,
the Vicar Apostolic of the London district, Nicholas Wiseman,
became the first Archbishop of Westminster, and was raised to the
Cardinalate.

One might conjecture about James II as one might about Queen
Mary. What would have happened if he had reigned for twenty
years instead of three? In the event, many Catholics came slowly to
accept the Protestant Settlement and the Hanoverian Succession as
accomplished facts, and in 1715 and 1745, attempts at a Stuart restoration were embarrassing to many of them—even so, if it had not

been for a failure of nerve at Derby in 1745, a Catholic Stuart monarchy would have been restored by a Scottish and northern English
army. By the end of the century, that doughty and devoted Ultra-
montane, John Milner, newly-consecrated Vicar Apostolic of the
Midland District, could describe George III in 1793 as "The assertor
of innocence and father of his country".

The Hanoverian dynasty that owed so much to the Dissenters
could hardly go on persecuting them, and in the eighteenth century
various Acts ingeniously took the pressure off them, and effectively
allowed them a place in the national life. The penal laws remained
in force against Catholics until the First and Second Relief Acts of
1778 and 1791. Until the First, any informer could collect £100 for
denouncing a Catholic priest; under the Second, Catholic churches
could once again be built, provided they were discreet and without
towers or steeples. John Milner moved quickly to build his new,
"beloved Chapel", in Winchester, which was consecrated on
December 5th 1792.

Not all recusants were the stuff of martyrs or saints; those who
were, are now properly exalted. Most continued to try to live their
lives in difficult circumstances, but one never knew when a blow
might fall. The last year of the life of Bishop Challoner saw the dev-
astating anti-Catholic Gordon Riots raging in London from June
2nd – 7th, 1780. He was able to take refuge with friends in Finchley,
and died the following January. His long episcopate, from 1758 to
1781, was one of continuous travelling around the south of England.
He dressed as a simple gentleman, carrying a collapsible mitre and
pastoral staff, to visit his scattered flock, who usually had to rely for
employment and protection on the remaining Catholic gentle and
noble families; Challoner's own mother was housekeeper to such
a family and became a convert, thus bringing up her son in the
Faith.

There were more Catholics in the north; communications were
difficult, many places fairly inaccessible. In the north-west beyond
the Mersey, the nearest Anglican bishop was in Chester, who,
pestered by the government, made Wigan into a sort of episcopal

outpost to keep watch over the papists. It was reasonably easy for the Blundells at Little Crosby and at Ince Blundell near Liverpool to get on with their lives, at some kind of peace with their neighbours, but facing very tense times on occasion. Nicholas Blundell had to serve his period of office as church warden of Sefton parish church, recusant or not, and his diaries are a detailed record of placid friendly relations with his neighbours. Priests said Mass in his house, but in 1708 a chapel was established in the cottage of one of his tenants, Ned Howerd, and Mass was said there secretly; it was never referred to as a chapel, but always as West Lane House, and it served the needs of the Catholics until 1847. In 1715, it was sensible for Nicholas Blundell to leave Little Crosby and go for a while to Flanders, taking his wife and daughters (he had no son). When he returned he was much preoccupied with trying to arrange good marriages for his daughters whom he had carefully educated with the Poor Clares at Gravelines (which was the first house founded by Mary Ward). According to John Bossy, he might have considered sending them on to the Bar Convent, but thought that the education provided there was too grand—a lot of Latin, and an unusual insistence on the study and performance of plays.

Over in Yorkshire, in the wild country inland from Whitby, Fr Nicholas Postgate could minister for thirty-four years before his arrest and execution in York in 1679. Baptisms, marriages and funerals took place clandestinely, "in a field", "under a tree", "in a close by the light of a lanthorn". In extremity, a lay-person could baptise and marriages could take place without the presence of a priest; funerals presented greater difficulty, as many Anglican clergy refused to bury known papists. Nicholas Blundell, in anger and disgust, created his own cemetery in the middle of a wood on his estate. Priests could never be referred to as such; the Mass was always "prayers", and one faces the fact that many Catholics were able to hear Mass only occasionally and rarely to receive Communion. This is what makes the account of Challoner's visitations so interesting, because his first purpose was to administer the Sacrament of Confirmation.

Everything conspired to keep religious life private and often secret. Mass must have been Low Mass; only important families had sets of vestments (Margaret Clitherow's house was used for storing vestments, kept to be carried wherever needed). Instruction in the Faith must have been about absolute essentials, and there were no widely used works of devotion until Challoner's *Garden of the Soul*, "a manual of Spiritual Exercises and Instructions for Christians who, living in the world, aspire to devotion". The first edition was published in 1740, and he continued to work on it for the rest of his life. I remember that Pope John XXIII was described as a "Garden of the Soul kind of Catholic", and the book has had an amazing circulation and impact. One also has to remember that Catholics were forbidden to use the Authorised Version of the Bible. For liturgy, they had the Tridentine Missal and the Latin Vulgate Bible. For an approved English text of the Bible, they had to wait. The importance of knowing enough Latin to understand the Vulgate was stressed time and again. Mary Ward had a particular determination about Latin. In a letter to Winifred Wigmore, then Novice Mistress in Naples, in 1627, she urged that, in the training of Novices, "what time can be found otherwise besides their prayer, let it be bestowed upon their Latin". The translations made at the beginning of the seventeenth century were expensive and bulky, and virtually not used. Nevertheless there was no new translation or revision after 1610, when the Rheims New Testament was added to the Douai Old Testament. After some attempts in the early eighteenth century, Challoner finally brought out what Newman described as "little short of a new translation", the New Testament in 1749 and the Old in 1750.

Cut off from public life, excluded from Oxford and Cambridge, obliged to keep "a low profile", English Catholics were also separated not only by distance but increasingly by all kinds of liturgical and artistic developments from the Catholic Continent. They were a small world of their own. There is a continuing argument about numbers, but it seems to be commonly acknowledged that Challoner's time was the low point. As a group, they survived. After the First Relief Act of 1778, the lifting of the more outrageous burdens was dependent on taking an Oath of Allegiance to the Hanoverian dynasty. The clergy were, by and large, dependent on the nobility and gentry for food and shelter. It is well known that it was John Milner, once he became a Vicar Apostolic, who kicked mightily against this lay control, and asserted the rights of the clergy, the rule of the bishops, and an unquestioning loyalty to the Holy See.

The French Revolution, the flight of so many French clergy to England, the extinction of the direct Stuart line with the death of Henry Stuart, Cardinal of York (who is buried in the Grotto under St Peter's in Rome as Henry IX of England), the irrefutable fact that the Hanoverians were here to stay (George III, in his kindly way, paid a pension to the Cardinal of York, who had lost most of his income as a result of Napoleon's conquest of Italy), all conspired to begin to bring about the beginning of the end of recusancy. Indisputably, however, it was the coming of the Irish that really changed things. From the middle of the eighteenth century, the standard economic rule that a high-level economy will suck in people from a low-level economy was operating, and it is impossible to calculate how many Irish have come to England since then; remarkably few people have not got Irish blood in them. By the 1820s, it became clear that it would not be possible to maintain the exclusion of Catholics from national life for much longer. George III had refused adamantly to contemplate equality for Catholics, and though George IV protested vigorously that he was being asked to break his coronation oath, it was under Wellington, the supreme realist, as Prime Minister, that Catholic Emancipation was passed in 1829.

Newman, in his famous sermon, "The Second Spring", preached on July 13th 1852, at the First Synod of the new hierarchy meeting at Oscott, romanticised the recusant world. Far from it being the case, he said, that "the past is out of date; the past is dead . . . The past has returned, the dead lives". He pictured the recusants surviving "in corners, and alleys, and cellars, and the housetops, or in the recesses of the country; cut off from the populous world around them and dimly seen, as if through a mist or in twilight, as ghosts flitting to and fro, by the high Protestants, the lords of the earth". It brought tears to the eyes of the bishops and clergy present, but he did warn them to remember the nature of the English Spring. The real recusant world was not like that. It had a "Low Church" mentality, positively against display and public emotion; it could be gritty. Such people knew little or nothing of Continental liturgical or musical developments, unless a few of them experienced them on the Grand Tour, and they were pretty scathing about foreigners. They accepted the Irish, who usually occupied lowly labouring positions, far more easily than they accepted Nicholas Wiseman, whose career had been lived on the Continent until his return as a Vicar Apostolic; his florid, romantic style embarrassed them greatly, and they were, in many cases, as affronted by his letter "From Outside the Flaminian Gate"—in which he announced his return to England as Archbishop of Westminster—as were their Protestant neighbours. The letter was read in Catholic churches on 13th October 1850. The next day, *The Times* described it as a "gross act of folly and impertinence . . . a daring assumption of power . . . an act which the laws of this country will never recognise".

Excluded from Oxford and Cambridge, the recusants had little understanding of Newman. One of the many graces in William Bernard Ullathorne was that this quintessential recusant priest always recognised Newman's uniqueness, and stood by him in times of great difficulty. It is no bad thing here to remember Ullathorne, whose life spanned much of the nineteenth century. Born in 1806, dying in 1889, he said on his death bed that "the last of the Vicars Apostolic is going". He grew up in a tiny Catholic community in Pocklington in the East Riding, which was served by a French priest, the Abbé Fidèle, who presumably was one of the émigré priests who did not return to France after the worst excesses of the Revolution were over. Ullathorne was of unbroken Catholic stock. His great-grandfather married a Miss Bynks, heiress of William Bynks and Anne More, and so was descended from the Saint and Martyr. Who could be better placed to remind Cardinal Manning, a convert, that he was a born Catholic and was a mitred bishop whilst "You were still an heretic"? He was from the old

Downside that sent most of its monks "on the mission", in his case, first to the convict settlements in Australia and then to the growing Irish communities in Coventry and Birmingham. Going from Vicar Apostolic to Bishop of Birmingham, Archbishop, "ad personam" in the last years of his life, he was the stalwart champion of Newman and other converts, offering them a place to live, and protecting them even though, sometimes, he did not understand them.

The recusant world, when it was able to build churches, mostly built in the style of the nonconformist chapels. Milner, with his passion for "antiquities", in other words things medieval, built in a "Gothick" style—but his carpenter's son, John Lingard, became one of the staunchest of the old-fashioned recusant clergy, very scornful of the new fancy ways. "Alas, alas the days of fun are over, and therefore, to be serious do accept Dr Wiseman's invitation. You may learn something new, at least how to wear purple stockings and silver buckles." On another occasion Lingard suggested as a subject for discussion (in February 1850), "How to send away those swarms of Italians who introduce their own customs here and by making religion ridiculous in the eyes of Protestants, prevent it spreading here." Lingard died in 1851, and therefore never had to accept the new ways—clergy wearing the "Roman Collar", addressed as "Father", kneeling to kiss bishops' rings. His stronghold was Ushaw, where priests are addressed to this day as "Mister".

The nuns in the Bar Convent had their hidden chapel built, by Thomas Atkinson, from 1765 to 1769—in a Continental Palladian style, shewing perhaps that, at that time they were far more in touch with Continental practices. They had to pretend to be a group of religiously-inclined spinsters earning a living from teaching girls, and those girls—daughters of local farmers and tradesmen—were perhaps unknowingly inducted into a Continental style, though the Mass was "Prayers" there as elsewhere.

Mary Ward and all her followers in England lived in the world just described, a recusant world which changed rapidly during the course of the nineteenth century, firstly with the coming of the Irish and then with the increasing number of converts. Cecilia Marshall was brought up a Catholic because her father was a *convert*. New styles in liturgy and architecture also came in, as the old austere chapels with their Low Mass gave way to the Gothic Revival, and the Continental-Italianate practices so beloved of Fr Faber of the London Oratory and so clearly despised by Lingard. Cecilia Marshall built her chapel at Ascot in the Gothic style, with an altar and reredos brought over from Bavaria. (No cathedral was built in London until the end of the century. From many designs submitted, Cardinal Vaughan chose the Byzantine proposals of Bentley so that there should not be a Gothic cathedral within sight of Westminster Abbey.)

The recusants were those who kept the Faith, when every kind of temptation was around them. No wonder the survivors were quietly proud. The Mass was central, and it was their devotion to it that saw them through. A perusal of the names of girls at St Mary's Ascot over its one hundred years shews many well-known recusant names. I have not counted, and it would be improper to do so. Many from other backgrounds have joined them. The school, established by the Institute, is in direct succession to the recusant world, not only in England but in exile. How much of this would come as a surprise to present or recent pupils? Does the inheritance, seen soberly and not romanticised by outsiders, matter?

3

English Catholic Education in the Nineteenth and Twentieth Centuries

The long recusant years ended in 1850 when Pope Pius IX "restored the Hierarchy". To be accurate, he created a new one. The pattern of the medieval dioceses, with additions, has remained the property of the Church of England. The Pope and his advisors fixed the new dioceses on different cities and towns that, at the time, had no Anglican connotations. This did not prevent the uproar of "Papal Aggression", and the Ecclesiastical Titles Bill, with its threat to imprison the new presuming prelates (never carried out). I came across a phrase recently, in relation to Catholic missionary activity in Russia, which describes the Orthodox reaction as fury at the trespass on their "canonical territory". This well describes the Anglican reaction in the mid-nineteenth century, though one can smile ruefully at the idea that England was their canonical territory.

With these new dioceses in place, it became possible to begin to sketch out, and slowly to make firm, parish boundaries. Missioners became parish priests, though many of the new parishes were served by religious orders who thought, and still think, of sending priests out on the mission. The diocese of Portsmouth was created only in 1882, by sub-dividing Southwark, and within it the parish at Ascot was created in 1887. This was soon put under the charge of the Franciscans, who were there until 1980.

The recusant world, perhaps never quite so diminished and dispirited everywhere as some have maintained, had been joined and was increasingly swamped by the flood of Irish immigration, which went almost entirely into the industrial conurbations.

Increasingly also, men and women of considerable education and sophistication from the upper reaches of the Church of England became Catholic. A consequence of all these three elements was the "mixed marriage", which raised questions about the education of the children thereof. The older practice, that the father decided the upbringing of sons, and the mother of daughters, ended with the strict ruling of Pius X in 1908, in the decree *Ne Temere*, which required all the children of mixed marriages to be brought up in the Catholic Faith as a condition of conducting and recognising the marriage.

The preoccupation can readily be seen to be with identity, its preservation and development in an essentially hostile and unsympathetic world. Identity meant a sense of separation, defensiveness and either pride in being different (and superior), or a feeling of being excluded, almost banned from national life. There was a great deal of uncharity all around. Was one a Roman Catholic, or worse, an RC, or was one a Catholic? There was considerable debate in the First Vatican Council as to how to describe the Church. The proposition "Holy, Roman, Catholic and Apostolic" was resisted doggedly by one of my heroes, Archbishop Ullathorne, on the grounds that it would play into Anglican hands. On the 24th March 1869, he moved that the Church should be described by the words "Holy, Catholic, Apostolic, and Roman Church." There was a debate on the placing of the last comma. He was anxious that "We may not seem to encourage in any way the tendencies of those who wish to qualify the word 'Catholic' by the word 'Roman'." On April 12th, the Fathers of Vatican I formally adopted his proposed description, unanimously, and so it came about that the very first words of the Dogmatic Decrees of the Council were promulgated by Ullathorne. This did not prevent Archbishop Benson of Canterbury from referring to the Catholic Church as the "Italian Mission". On the other side, Cardinal Manning forbade Catholic young men from attending Oxford or Cambridge Universities in case their Faith might be contaminated. In 1896 Leo XIII pronounced Anglican Orders to be "utterly null and void".

Mary Ward (1585 - 1645),
Foundress of the Institute of the
Blessed Virgin Mary. Portrait at
Augsburg, artist unknown.

Mary Ward in her pilgrim's clothes, 1621.
Portrait at Augsburg, artist unknown.

Maria ist Aᵒ.1621 von Trier nacher Rom in pilgrams kleider zu fueß gereist

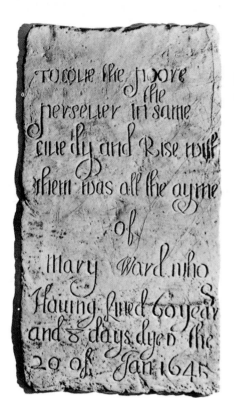

To loue the poore
the perseuer in same
cue dly and Rise with
them was all the ayme
of
Mary ward who
Hauing liued 60 years
and 8 days dyed the
20 of Jan 1645

Mary Ward's gravestone in the porch of Osbaldwick Church, near York.

Gravestones of the 'English Ladies' in Augsburg. One is thought to be that of Mary Poyntz.

The First Girls at St Mary's Ascot, 1885. Cecilia Marshall, front row, extreme right.

School Group, 1899.

Mother Mary Hewitt, the third mistress in charge, with two girls and possibly an unidentified lay teacher in the Long Drive.

Mother Cecilia Marshall, Mother Vincent Duhamel and the
school choir, about 1900.

Mother Ignatius with school coach party en route to Lourdes, year unknown.
(Photograph by courtesy of Miss Rachel Blayney and Mr J. M. Beveridge.)

Mother Ignatius Beveridge reading the coach lists outside the Concert Hall on the Feast of St Aloysius (Aloy Day), 1937.

Mother Ignatius and Mother Perpetua, 1962, at the home of the Orchards.

Overleaf: The reordered Chapel.

St. Mary's Convent, South Ascot.   The Studio.   16785.

The first Art Studio from a card sent by Mother Ignatius, January 15th 1926, to B. Hannay: "Thank you very much for your letter and good wishes. I hope you and Anne have had lovely holidays . . . This term you must break a record by not getting a single cold. Much love from us all."

Muriel Davenport (later Mother Campion).

It is easy to understand why schools and schooling were seen to be central to the purposes of preserving, developing and extending the Faith. Parish priests worked unceasingly to create parochial schools, paid for by the pennies of the poor, in order to match those run by the British and Foreign Schools Society for the Noncon-formists and by the National Society of the Church of England. It was not until 1847 that the Catholic schools were able to claim a share in the Privy Council grant that the other two had been receiv-ing since 1833. The Catholic Poor School Committee was estab-lished in 1847 to exercise a general supervisory care over the financial and administrative interests of the schools as a whole. (This became, in more recent times, the Catholic Education Council, recently reorganised, with greatly extended duties as the Catholic Education Service.) To accept government money required open-ness to inspection by Her Majesty's Inspectors, who until the gen-eral reorganisation in the 1870 Education Act had to be Catholic themselves. (In fact, even in modern times, very few Catholics were appointed. I myself, in 1960, was regarded with some apprehension by my territorial superior on my first posting to the North West—I was advised that Catholic education was decidedly second rate, and that once the news got round that I was a Catholic, priests and nuns would try to beguile me to their underhand purposes.)

The teaching of religion in these schools was always a separate matter, the concern of diocesan priests, who seemed to have con-centrated on ensuring that children had a basic, perhaps elementary knowledge of the Faith. The Penny Catechism was the text to live by. An entry in the Log Book of a school in Wigan in 1884 captures this perfectly. In a beautiful copperplate hand the headmaster wrote: "Today we had religious inspection. Some of the children knew why God had made them. Others did not, but they know now."

The provision of such schools was seen to be far more important than the building of churches or cathedrals. For example, Cardinal Manning refused to be diverted from building schools for the poor into building a cathedral at Westminster. These elementary schools were for boys and girls together, "all-age", taking the children from the beginning of compulsory attendance to wherever the school leaving age was fixed as time went by. Architecturally, many of them were "three-deckers", based as all such were on the designs used by the London School Board. They were often overcrowded and poorly equipped. The financing of them remained a source of controversy until the general settlement of the 1944 Act, which finally incorporated Catholic schooling, with its own character and rights preserved, into the national system. Until then the tensions between the bishops and local and national authorities were often bitter. The fear was that the acceptance of State money would erode diocesan control and thereby diminish the teaching of the Faith. On the non-Catholic side, there was an equally bitter hostility towards using public money to help an alien body—"Rome on the Rates" was a major issue in local elections at the beginning of this century. The perceptive reader will see analogies in the present position of Muslims.

The part played by religious orders in this story is enormous. The activities of the male orders were to be found more in providing secondary, grammar or "Public" schooling. Many of these were unavoidably fee-paying, day or boarding. Their achievement was great, but in truth not so great as that of women Religious, certainly in quantity. There was an extraordinary multiplicity of orders and congregations of nuns, active across the whole educational range. All, with one exception—the IBVM—of Continental foundation, they worked so often in city-centre, slum conditions. Their devotion was extraordinary, and they risked a great deal of public hostility—convents aroused ignorant and foolish suspicion of dark deeds and of women imprisoned against their will. The work of the Notre Dame, the Ursuline, the Holy Child, the Sisters of Mercy and of so many other congregations justifies the view that they were the backbone of Catholic education of this country until the disturbance and disorientations in the aftermath of the Second Vatican Council, which have in many cases almost obliterated what they did.

On such a broad canvas, the IBVM occupies only a small part. Its greatest achievement throughout the nineteenth century was to maintain, indeed to preserve and develop the Bar Convent School in York. That this was done at some cost has been shewn already; the loss of independence, supervision by the local bishop, the perceived necessity to live an enclosed life cut them off from the Continental mainstream, until the reunion of 1911.

Mother Cecilia Marshall seems to have found it difficult to accept that York was, so-to-speak, fully one hundred per cent paid-up. She used the word "Yorky" in a pejorative sense to describe elements that she did not like, and even when she became Superior of York as well as Ascot in 1925, and first Provincial of the English Province, seemed to view York somewhat distantly. It was in the far North, taking in different sorts of girls, and, apparently, harsher and more rigid within the convent in its approach to the religious life. Sisters at Ascot seem to have felt that to be sent to York was a form of exile. Writing on March 7th 1950 to Mother Campion Davenport in Rome Mother Cecilia said,

> I shall re-read the Loreto customs but they will be very Yorky as they were founded from York after York had gone under the Bishop and changed so much. I don't quite know what Mother Helen means by "making York the centre of the Institute". Of course it is the eldest house and much to be venerated but it did go away from the original design . . . they adopted enclosure, went under that bishop and were much influenced by their chaplains who were secular priests.

Nevertheless, it was York that tried to establish a house in Cambridge for Catholic women students in the university, so that they might live there in the days when women were first asserting their right to higher education. The attempt failed, and the Sisters changed to running a school there for day and boarding girls. The lineage of St Mary's Ascot is to Hampstead, and from Hampstead to Ascot. York's succession from Mary Ward is via Frances Bedingfield,

Ascot's is via Mary Poyntz, the youngest of her first disciples.

Not by a long way were the nuns of the early days, in any Order, professionally trained teachers. Many, perhaps most of them, had no formal training except in the schooling they had received, usually as girls in their own convent schools. This was true of Mother Cecilia Marshall herself, but it was she who recognised that her Sisters of the next generation would need higher education and professional training. Prompted and encouraged by Cardinal Bourne, she joined with Mother Dymphna Fox of the Holy Child Congregation and Mother Declan of the Sacred Heart to establish the Convents Schools' Association in 1918. This in turn was to become the Association of Teaching Religious. It became policy to send selected Sisters to university or college. The IBVM usually sent them to one of the colleges of London University though some went to other universities, proceeding after taking their degrees to professional teacher training. A poignant obituary notice in the school magazine (1992 – 93) of Sister Cecily Heller describes how she, as Maria Magdalena Heller, an Austrian Jewish refugee, entered the IBVM Novitiate at Ascot in 1939 and was then sent to Reading University, where she took a First in Physics and Mathematics. She hated teaching these subjects, and returned to her first love, Music. Sister Cecily was a most distinguished musician, and a dedicated teacher of piano and organ. Others were sent to be trained in Domestic Science, particularly with the establishment of the school at Errollston in 1936—of which more later. Though they wore the religious habit, they were able to move quite freely—part of Mother Cecilia's enlightened views.

When Mother Ignatius, headmistress at Ascot from 1921 to 1949, was invited to attend a meeting of the Headmasters' Conference, this was a symbolic acceptance of the Sisters into the main stream of independent education. I have not found the date; it must be somewhere in the archives of H. M. C. Her nephew, Mr J. M. Beveridge, surmises that this came about through her friendship with Dom Paul Nevill, the headmaster of Ampleforth.

The Sisters at York, for all their apparent limitations, did teach non fee-paying as well as fee-paying pupils, and were a force in the life of the city. Their school was the only witness to the work of Mary Ward in this country for the whole of the eighteenth and most of the nineteenth centuries. When Ascot was established, one or two Sisters were sent into the nearby parish school, but Mother Cecilia, who was headmistress of St Mary's from 1904 to 1921, and the all-pervading influence through to her death in 1960, was content to build up one school, and to make it very specially her own. In her day, and until the 1980s, fees were not high, and if the school became exclusive, it was not by being expensive, but rather by drawing on a fairly restricted circle of families who sent their children to it through the generations. Only in the 1960s was the nature of the intake widened, and even now it is a school for only 340 girls, with no real possibility of further expansion without drastic changes of all kinds. Such matters have to be kept in mind when one returns to Mary Ward's determination to do all the little she could for God, and for England. Her conviction that the survival of the Faith in England lay with women, as mothers and first educators of their children, could be linked to Cecilia Marshall's desire to establish a school whose pupils would be so well loved and cared for that, for all its exclusiveness, they would leave it to be religiously responsible mothers, and also capable of leadership. This was her justification of Ascot. There had to be a "best", by which the other schools of the Institute could be measured.

The most dramatic, and to many distressing, development in Catholic education in the last twenty-five years has been the withdrawal of religious Orders and Congregations from schools and colleges. The Renewal called for by Vatican II had some unforeseen and calamitous consequences, with so many departures of priests and religious into "laicisation" that the fabric of the system was endangered, and rather precipitate moves had to be made towards new structures, chiefly concerned with handing over to lay control. A marked falling-off in vocations, combining with the departure of so many, has left Orders and Congregations with no alternative but to retreat, and to accept secular leadership. This is as marked at

Ascot as anywhere else. From a Community of sixty-five and more up to the 1960s, with most of the teaching in the school in its hands, a position has been reached in which no Headship of an academic department is held by a Sister and their role is now largely managerial and pastoral. The Governors are prepared to accept that the day will come—perhaps in 1997—when they must appoint a lay head. The question looms as to how the mind and spirit of Mary Ward will continue to pervade every aspect of the education provided. I became increasingly aware that, in writing this book, I was writing a history of two, admittedly closely connected, schools. The first dated from 1885 to the headship of Sister Bridget, when all teaching was in the hands of the Sisters; in Sister Bridget's later years there began to emerge the second school, where teaching was progressively transferred to an ever larger number of lay staff, with all that that implied.

This is a far cry from those earlier years, "the Ascot of the Nuns", when not only the teaching but every aspect of the support services was carried out by the Sisters. It has already been pointed out that fees could be kept low because none of the Sisters received salaries or payment. The lay Sisters were, so-to-speak, unpaid domestic servants. Apart from the fact that lay teachers were brought in part-time, for example for music, or appointed for the year, for example in physical education, there was no full-time lay member of staff until 1961. The school was "snobby", as it was described to me, but with the proper rider that so were other similar schools, and that this was part of the culture of the times; it was, as one distinguished Old Girl put it, a "servant-employing culture" from which most of the girls came. They, therefore, saw nothing odd in a school reflecting their homes. The school itself, inward-looking and little affected by the outside world—it hoped to give a sound and careful education, but never remotely claimed to innovate—was very like the rest of Catholic England in the first half of this century. The Church itself, there and elsewhere, had what has been described as a fortress mentality. It viewed the secular world as hostile and wicked, and called on it to "return" to the Faith from which it had wandered so far. This way of thinking reached its peak in the Pontificate of Pius XII (1939 – 58). Within it, provided the rules were kept, one was safe. It was an event for Catholics to take part in public life, to be in the Honours List—these things were mentioned—and on the other hand the reception of well-known people into the Church, usually by Father D'Arcy, S J, was a feature of the times. His reception of Frank Pakenham in due course brought his eldest daughter Antonia, not then a Catholic, to St Mary's and established a considerable connection with this family.

Some of the rigours required of Catholics do need to be recalled: the ban on attending non-Catholic religious services—permission was required even to go to a funeral; the ban on saying the Lord's Prayer with non-Catholic Christians; the cold rigidities of mixed marriages—in the Liverpool Archdiocese in the 1920s and 1930s, they took place in the church porch. There was certainly a Path to Rome; there was also a path from it. There was an extraordinary deference to ecclesiastical rank, frequently recorded for example in the Ascot magazine on the occasions when Archbishop (later Cardinal) Godfrey, whether as Apostolic Delegate or as Archbishop of Westminster, stayed there.

The whole Church began to change dramatically when Pius XII died and John XXIII was elected. The Second Vatican Council intended a complete review of every aspect of Church life; what it did not intend was the earthquake that shook the lives of priests, religious and laity. In 1968, Paul VI issued *Humanae Vitae*. One would expect that this encyclical would have had a major impact on Ascot but if it did, then I have found no written evidence. I have been told that the teaching Sisters were called together and instructed that there was to be no formal mention of it.

In 1965 the Labour government, by issuing Circular 10/65, signalled its intention to bring to an end the tripartite arrangement of secondary education brought in by the 1944 Act—grammar, technical and "modern"—and to proceed to introduce secondary comprehensive schooling. From that day onwards, secondary education has been a battlefield. It is apt enough—not entirely true, but apt enough—to quote Matthew Arnold's last lines in "Dover Beach":

> For the world . . .
> Hath really neither joy, nor love, nor light,
> Nor certitude, nor peace, nor help for pain;
> And we are here as on a darkling plain
> Swept with confused alarms of struggle and flight,
> Where ignorant armies clash by night.

It will be remembered that Matthew Arnold was one of Her Majesty's Inspectors.

From 1978 until 1990, the schools' world was divided simply between maintained and independent; now there is "opting out", and grant-maintained status, whereby hitherto maintained schools can obtain independence from local authority control and move to direct financing from central government. In any case, all schools, whatever their status, now receive individual budgets with the responsibility for managing them. These vast changes have had a profound effect on Catholic education; bishops are divided in attitude, for example, to "opting out", and fear a diminishing control over the Catholic system. Furthermore, in April 1993, post-sixteen institutions were freed from local control; for Catholics, this affects sixth-form colleges. To all of this, add the decline in numbers in the Catholic school population. The contraceptive pill, Papal Encyclical or not, is affecting Catholics, it would seem, to more or less the same degree as the rest. At the time of writing, there are only two Catholic independent schools that have a substantial waiting list, so that they can insist on an entirely Catholic entry. St Mary' School Ascot is one of them. The opening of the Mary Ward Court in 1992 was the most challenging move by the headmistress and governors to resist the growing national trend for girls to leave their single sex schools at sixteen, in order to go into coeducational post-sixteen provision. The battle is on to hold at Ascot these highly-motivated and intelligent young women, who can contribute so much.

4

The Earlier History of St Mary's School Ascot, 1885 to 1921

It is now that the particular problems present themselves in approaching the writing of this narrative. The chief of these, and the most obvious, is the lack of written evidence, especially for the earliest years. A small religious community had no particular reason for keeping well-arranged, chronologically-sorted documents. I was told that the Ascot archives were at the Bar Convent in York. A visit there brought important conversations with Sister Gregory and Sister Agatha, and the Archive Room is a most interesting place; but Ascot was, so-to-speak, two large cardboard boxes, containing a small miscellany of fairly unimportant papers. Back at the school itself, there was some bewilderment as to whether anything else was likely to be found. For example, the reports by H. M. Inspectors in 1931 and 1953 were discovered, but Sister Bridget had to admit that on the day that she ceased to be headmistress in 1976, the last report, from 1968, was "in the third drawer down on the right of my desk. I remember that clearly, but I have no idea what happened after that". If the reader is tempted to say that, surely a copy must be in the archives of the library of what used to be the Department of Education and Science and is now the Department for Education, all that I can reply is that it has moved buildings across London, and the library and archives are not yet rearranged. In addition, as I have explained already, the School was lost sight of by the Department, and records were impossible to trace.

A further, and to any historian an every-day but nevertheless in-furiating circumstance, was that if and when any record was kept, it reflected the interests of those who kept it. It was not written to meet the needs of a later enquirer from a different age. This was put so much more dramatically and grandly by Thomas Carlyle, in his book *Past and Present* (1843) that it is worth quoting. He was referring to a medieval chronicler, Jocelyn of Brakelond, who recorded lovingly what mattered to him in the life of Abbot Samson of St Edmundsbury round about 1200. Carlyle rails and bemoans:

> These clear eyes of Jocelyn looked on the bodily presence of King John; the very John Sansterre, or Lackland, who signed Magna Carta afterwards in Runnymead. Lackland, with a great retinue, boarded once for the matter of a fortnight, in St Edmundsbury, daily in the very eyesight, palpable to the very fingers of our Jocelyn: O Jocelyn, what did he say, what did he do; how looked he, lived he—at the very lowest, what coat or breeches had he on? Jocelyn is obstinately silent. Jocelyn marks down what interests him, entirely deaf to us . . . It is Jocelyn's manner with all things; and it is men's manner and men's necessity. How intermittent is our good Jocelyn, marking down, without eye to us, what he finds interesting.

At a very modest level, this was the case in the York Archive. Someone unknown, perhaps more than one person, made some jottings from 1890 (that is five years after the school began) through to 1918, of what interested her (I presume), with an innocent disregard for the big world outside. For a first example, in 1890 the main event was that "Sister Benedicta, Sister M. Gertrude and Cecilia Marshall went to Wiesbaden to consult an oculist for C. M.'s eyes. She came back to school on January 6th after her father's death and decided to enter the convent. She was made a ward in Chancery." Two years after these jottings end, came the first issue of the school magazine in 1920, and this, for every year up to the present, is the only continuous historical record of the school's life. Until fairly recently, the editor was always an IBVM Sister. It is a faithful chronicle, and I have analysed it under all possible headings. Its very orthodoxy makes it reliable, if sometimes dull. It reflects, often innocently but precisely, the official attitude of its times. When it is not a chronicle, it is a mirror of some of the written work of the girls that met with approval. It was never critical in an evaluative sense, but only of the performance and behaviour of some girls at some times. Therefore, there has had to be a heavy reliance on what people have been willing to talk about.

So far as has been possible, the attempt has been made to see the school through its headmistresses, but the first three are decidedly shadowy—Veronica Lund (1885 to 1891), Gertrude Blagden (1891 to 1898), and Barbara Hewett (1898 to 1904). In all probability, they were simply "teachers-in-charge". It was Mother M. Joseph Edwards who, as Superior, controlled what happened.

There were only nineteen pupils in 1885 and thirty-nine in 1904. When Cecilia Marshall became headmistress in 1905, matters become easier. Mother Cecilia lives on in the hearts and minds of many people to this day; and then there is a considerable amount of information about Mother Ignatius (1921 to 1949). Mother Mercedes presents problems, incidentally revealing one of the difficulties in using the magazine, namely that one has to wait until someone dies in order to gain access to the information in her Obituary—Mother Mercedes resigned the headship in 1956 but died in 1989. Matters become entirely different with the headship of Mother Bridget and her successors. Even so, it has to be said that we are dealing with a group of Religious, living together in one community, and with a clear chain of command. The Provincial, the Superior and the headmistress were all together. Technically, and in reality, the Superior was in charge of the school, as Principal, and signed all the girls' reports, allocated Sisters to teaching duties, and dealt, along with the Provincial, with all financial matters. There was no Bursar, accounting was of the simplest, and there were very few salaries to be paid—until 1961, only to temporary part-time teachers.

In 1961, Mlle Arlette Kalflèche was appointed to be the first full-time lay teacher, slowly to be joined over the years by a growing number of such members of staff. Nevertheless, they were on individual contracts of the simplest possible nature. They were required to teach and to undertake no other duties whatsoever; they were lovingly cared for and treated with great courtesy, but quite excluded from the pastoral care of the girls and the general life of the school. The only other lay person of importance seems to have been Miss Frith, a personal friend of Mother Cecilia's, residing in a "grace and favour" house on the estate, presiding in grand dignity at the mealtimes of the lay teachers in a separate room from the Sisters, and driving Mother Cecilia by motor-car wherever she wished to go. The transition to what President Harding called "normalcy" began in the time of Sister Emmanuel (1976 to 1982). She is now Sister Gillian, one of the many members of the IBVM who have changed habits, in more senses than one, since Vatican II.

In the later years of the nineteenth century, and well into this, there were men and women who wished to bring something new into education. Some, but not all, were personally wealthy and were able to use their own money selflessly; others were highly successful persuaders to bring in other people's money. Almost always, the sources were industrial, the "dark Satanic Mills". Cecilia Marshall was precisely from this world. (Sir Hubert Parry, who set Blake's words to music, was Sister Gillian's and Sister Mark Orchard's great-uncle.) She was wealthy, and succeeded through legal battles in getting control of her money, which came from the Yorkshire woollen mills—like so many, her grandfather moved away from his factories, in his case, to live in Patterdale in the Lake District. At Ascot, it seems clear that, even as the years went by and she was less and less directly involved in the school—in later years mainly on her Feast Day, St Cecilia's on November 22nd—yet everyone knew very well that she was the fount and origin of money. She was not a major national figure, not a Miss Beale or a Miss Buss. With the conventional and limited education she had had in the first years at Ascot, she was not bursting with new ideas, eager to break through boundaries. She was in no sense an original educational thinker; she had no desire to innovate. She was a late-Victorian lady of means, who accepted the social culture of her times. The "two-tier" IBVM was acceptable to her, and she never moved to make fundamental changes. She felt most at ease with other people in similar comfortable circumstances. Even as a Religious, she kept the good taste of her times, and had the tender gracious manners of a lady, dispensing kindness and gifts—in the most austere days of the Second World War, she handed out, bestowed is perhaps a better word, chocolate, sweets and fruit on the great feasts of the Church.

She had found at Ascot a home, what is more a religious home; after all, her own greatest struggle was to become a Catholic Religious. Her family were certain that if she succeeded she would take the family fortune with her into the IBVM. And so she did. She used it first to build and furnish the glorious Chapel in 1896, the year she was clothed. Ascot became everything that she wanted, the life of a Catholic Religious in a place that was home. Home meant stability and security; faith meant, according to Father Corbishley,

> a serenity, a joy, a wholesomeness and a spontaneity that could spring only from a sense of complete psychological satisfaction . . . In years to come, her letters to her daughters manifest a loving concern for the interests, problems and achievements of each of them . . . She was able to develop in her community, and in the Province as a whole, that remarkable family spirit which is at once Mary Ward's own way of government and the fruit of her own experience . . . She had come to find lasting happiness and satisfaction within the walls of Ascot.

Devoted as she was to Mary Ward, proud that she might be called a Jesuitess, historically she—and the IBVM of the time—seem to me to be disconnected from much of the essential nature of the original purpose. It is easily understandable that in the 17th and 18th centuries, the Sisters had to accept a conventualised life; they would not have survived otherwise. But, by the late 19th century, with various movements towards women's liberation gathering force, one might ponder as to whether a Cecilia Marshall might have struck out more strongly for a more open return to the Foundress's intentions. True enough, Mother Cecilia brought in some flexibility, in personal freedom of movement, for example, but she and the Sisters lived in a Convent, and wore a beautiful but elaborate habit, and there was an ever-increasing amount of deference to her. Without wishing to hurt or offend, I see her as being much more in a long line of impressive Lady Abbesses, than as a fighting spirit out in the world in the Mary Ward sense.

By the time that she died, there were over two hundred girls at Ascot, but this still made it a small school. If anything stands out irrefutably from the magazine, it is that the school was a family, cared for, watched over, "waited on hand and foot" as my mother would say. But so marked by the experience were most girls that, if they had families of their own, they were determined to send their own daughters to Ascot. This, above everything else, was Mother Cecilia's achievement. She had helpers, and as she became increasingly prominent in the affairs of the Institute as a whole, she relied on faithful lieutenants. Mother Ignatius Beveridge was her chief assistant from 1913 until 1949, and it is clear that they were a very successful partnership. I am sure that there was iron in Mother Cecilia's beautiful velvet glove; I do not think that Mother Ignatius—"the Iron Duchess", or more delightfully "Bomber Command"—wore gloves. She was the capable executive, the disciplinarian; a few girls were terrified of her, a few saw a kind and gentle side, though usually after they had left. Antonia Fraser/Pakenham looks back on her with great affection; Antonia was seen as someone who needed special attention and she got it.

There is nothing in the earlier Ascot of the scholarship, the devotion grounded in deep knowledge, the profundity of Mary Ward's first companions, or the sense of mission to keep the Faith shining bright in a hostile world that characterises so much of the history of the Bar Convent. The first Ascot was a genteel, loving and kindly small school, and Cecilia Marshall was a lady of means who became a Religious. The school has become nationally important and internationally well-known only in more recent years.

The story of the beginnings of the school at Ascot are well-enough known, but had better be repeated. Petronella Barrett, the daughter of a Dublin doctor, entered the Institute in Augsburg as a convert. She had gone there first as a lay teacher of English. When professed, she was sent back to Ireland. This proved to be an unhappy experience, and so she came to Gloucester in 1862 to open a house and a school there. Petronella became Mother Ignatius at Gloucester, which was not a successful enterprise. The community was not well-received in a town they came to regard as "too Protestant". So it removed itself to Haverstock Hill, going up towards Hampstead. This was in 1872, and four years later the Sisters moved to England's Lane in Hampstead itself. At that time, Hampstead was a separate village from London and, one would have thought, healthily removed from the smoke and fogs of the city. When every household, every factory and every public building was heated by coal fires, the soot and grime blackened the brickwork and fouled the air. A significant social movement, especially by the well-to-do, was to escape "the vile city", and to live as far out in the country as the spreading railway network allowed. The most idealistic expression of all this was the Garden City movement, symbolised by Letchworth. Apparently, not even Hampstead—where a garden suburb was later to be built—was healthy enough for one member, Frances Macdonough, and so it was decided to lease a house in Ascot, to which members of the community might retire for rest or convalescence.

Ascot was chosen because a Dominican priest, Fr Portley, who occasionally said Mass for a small group of Catholics there, knew Mother Joseph Edwards, who had been a novice in the new community at Gloucester, and had succeeded Mother Ignatius Barrett in 1869. I have been told that she came over from the Loreto Branch, and that she was never accepted entirely as "one of us". Fr Portley persuaded her to move to Ascot, where their first rented house proved unsuitable, and so some land nearby was bought. This in its turn was found to be unsuitable and another site, of thirty acres, was acquired as a result of the disinterested actions of their solicitor, Mr Walshe. The architect, Goldie, was the son of the man who designed the hideous church of St Wilfrid that stands, presumptuously, opposite York Minster.

With considerable help from the powerful IBVM house at Nymphenburg, then the Mother House of the Roman Branch and the residence of the Mother General, the new building was put up, and the first Mass said there on August 5th 1885, by Bishop Virtue, the first Catholic Bishop of Portsmouth. It was dedicated to Our Lady of the Snows, a title of Mary to which Mary Ward had been particularly devoted. The move did not cure Frances Macdonough, who died shortly afterwards. There is some difficulty in establishing the names of the first members of the IBVM who went to Ascot. I think the list is : Mothers Joseph Edwards, Paul Wyte, Magdalen Gremion, Veronica and Gabrielle Lund, and Gertrude Blagden, with Sisters Antony Kane, Dominic Davies, Agatha Wheeler, Baptist Montgomery, and Crescentia Drexel. I think I have got this right, but Corbishley has a shorter list. Mother Veronica was to be the first teacher-in-charge of the school, and Mother Gertrude Blagden the second.

Mother Joseph Edwards might best be described as determined, no-nonsense, staunch, and on occasion, outspoken. The truth of the Loreto connection seems to be that she had joined the IBVM in Augsburg, and had been "lent" to the Loreto House in Ireland, then reclaimed and sent, still a novice, to Gloucester; professed, she went to take charge in north London and thence to Ascot. Her determination to secure proper recognition for Mary Ward had led her, on one occasion, to tell a powerful Roman Cardinal that she would accept no constitutions for her House until Mary Ward was recognised fully and publicly as the Foundress of the Institute. It was for this reason that she established a House in Rome, from which she intended to exert pressure on the Holy See. She it was who made the move to Ascot, she saw to it that Mother Catherine Chambers wrote the first modern, authoritative two-volume life of the Foundress, and she was a true surrogate mother to Cecilia Marshall. She was not a person to be trifled with.

The new building remains still the heart of the school. At first, and indeed for many years up to the 1960s, it housed the community as well as the small number of girls in the school. The first extensions were in 1896, above all the chapel built with Cecilia Marshall's money. The magnificently ornate altar arrived from Nuremburg, where it had been an exhibit in one of those great exhibitions that were a marked feature of the second half of the nineteenth century. A beautifully laid out estate was created; the acid soil is right for rhododendrons and azaleas, and it is a glory in Spring. The district is no longer sparsely built on, but has become one of the wealthiest residential areas in England; the high walls, steel fences and occasionally visible armed guards tell of the presence—though largely invisible—of native and foreign potentates.

The first ten years at Ascot were hard, with little or no money, great discomfort, and much improvisation. After the first extensions in 1896 more came in 1906: chapel, dormitories, infirmary, extended kitchen; and again more building in 1914, in 1926, in 1935 and on many occasions after this. In 1887, the Bishop of Portsmouth established a parish at Ascot which was to be served by the Franciscans until 1980. Sisters from the Community provided headteachers and teachers for its school until 1960; this was their chief activity in the neighbourhood and they did not venture further afield. There was a Catholic presence in Ascot, and as a priest said at the very first Mass, "Once more the Angelus will ring out over the land".

St Mary's was a very small school for girls from the age of about 10 to 15 or 16. It taught more than the lady-like skills, but not so much more; when Cecilia Marshall, having made her final profession in 1898, began to teach in the school, she was responsible for music and needlework. The teaching was in the hands of the Mothers who were of good social standing. It became customary to bring lay people in on temporary contracts, particularly to teach physical education. The care of the everyday lives of the girls, of their clothes and shoes, and the preparation of their meals, was the work of the lay Sisters who often were either Irish or German—I have been told of one Sister who arrived from Germany, with her boat and train tickets pinned to her habit, because she did not speak any English at all.

The Irish connection was always somewhat ambivalent. England was Protestant or pagan, unreliable and hostile to the Faith. The first three Bishops of Portsmouth were Irish and, it would seem, decidedly suspicious of English candidates for the priesthood. Ireland was safe, but essentially a peasant culture, with only a small Catholic professional class. Therefore it was a good source of lay Sisters but, as Sister Magdalen Ingram so delightfully put it to me about Mothers Ignatius, Mercedes and Perpetua, it was a little difficult to explain how they came to Ascot—"the Lawler sisters [that is, Mercedes and Perpetua] sort of blew in from Ireland."

Only in the mid-1920s did the school pass the one hundred mark. Parents were not looking for an academic education; they were not ambitious for their daughters except in marriage terms. Lady Antonia Fraser recalls recurrent exhortations never to marry Protestants. Otherwise there was the call to the religious life, and the school magazine records, year in year out, the vocations of Old Girls to the IBVM or other Orders. The last vocation to the IBVM from Ascot itself was of Wendy Orchard, now Sister Mark. In 1920, thirty-five years on, the first school magazine recorded that there were "three new resident mistresses—Miss Humphrys (Newnham College, Cambridge), Miss Birmingham (Queen Alexandra House, London), Mlle Mulquin (Paris). They were to teach English, Physical Culture and French, "now that the school is so big". The full number on roll was ninety.

Cecilia Marshall became headmistress in 1904, Superior in 1913, Superior of both Ascot and York in 1925 and Provincial in 1929. Contrary to all known Canon Law, she was Provincial and Superior for the rest of her life. There can be no doubting the all-pervasiveness of her influence; she came to be important in the affairs of the Institute as a whole throughout Europe. Her greatest challenge had been to win the battle to enter the Institute; but from then onwards it does not seem that she met problems that tested her to her limit. Her spiritual life was not hammered and beaten into shape. It has been said she built up around her a community of agreeable and compliant women; one had to be "beautiful, musical or aristocratic" to be in her good books. Others were "exiled to other Houses and schools".

Sister Bridget recalls gathering her courage to ask her why Ascot always came first in her thoughts, when as Provincial she had the care of all the Houses and schools. She replied that every organisation must have a top, by which the best could be recognised. To her, Ascot was the measure for all the schools of the Institute. As quotations from her private correspondence with Mother M. Campion Davenport have shewn, she always had a colder view of York, which had strayed from the true path during the nineteenth century. Nor did she view the Loreto branch of the Institute with much affection. She did not particularly like the German preponderance in the Institute in her day, but she did recognise it as the stem rather than as a branch. She attracted the admiration and love of pupils, and many photographs shew this. As the years went by, places in the school were filled increasingly by the daughters of her pupils, so that entry became ever more difficult for anyone else. Perhaps only after her death was it possible to make breaks with this pattern, and to admit fully from a wider world.

It has already been pointed out how thin the evidence from the early days is, not much more than diary jottings. As an example, one can look at a few entries for the 1890s:

"In 1892, elementary school building over at St Francis' Church was begun."

"1894 St Francis' School opened, Sister Magdalen Gremion and Sister M. Ignatius Poulton sent to work in it. Sister Agatha Wheeler who came as a maid from Gloucester with the nuns and afterwards entered, died."

"1895 building of the chapel begun by C. Marshall. She reached the age of 21 and could do what she liked. Old chapel turned into classroom, refectory enlarged, 2 dormitories and bathroom built, 3 piano rooms etc. Reverend Mother M. Joseph ordered a change of air."

"1896 Chapel dedicated . . . christening of the Bell . . . C. M. clothed March 25th."

"1897 Mother General thanked Rev. Mother publicly for founding

House in Rome and there was a consultation on calling Mary Ward foundress. New altar arrived, had been in the Nuremburg Exhibition. Packed in many boxes, and whilst watching the unpacking on a wet night Sister M. Ignatius Poulton caught a severe cold which turned to pneumonia."

"1898 Sister M. Barbara Hewitt appointed Mistress of Schools in place of Sister M. Gertrude Blagden . . . frightful epidemic of influenza . . . Sister Cecilia's profession . . . About this time Queen Victoria visited Ascot and went to Lady Ponsonby's House, her grounds adjoining the Convent. [This is most probably Gilmuire.] The Queen very graciously turned and bowed to the Sisters and children who went out to see her."

"1899 Sister M. Ignatius Poulton too ill and in too much disgrace to continue as Novice Mistress, so sent to London." [What on earth did she do?]

"1901 A most eventful year. Rev. Mother M. Joseph died on March 22nd . . . Many changes . . . Bonnets discarded, cloaks introduced, opposition everywhere. 1902 Father Thurston S. J. gave the retreat. It was very severe."

The death of Queen Victoria is not recorded, nor the Boer War, nor the death of Edward VII, though in 1910 Sister M. Cecilia Marshall "not being well, went for a change to Homburg". In 1914, it is mentioned that war had broken out and that "meetings for sewing opened during the holidays". In spite of the War, many of the nuns travelled around Europe, especially to Rome. In 1916 "Sister Consiglio, who was German, was in Ireland when she was caught by the War. She was brought over to Ascot to work in the House . . . She did not suit the work and the work did not suit her." She did eventually do some good work in music. These fragments eventually ended in 1918, for which the only entry is that "Father Gartlan gave the retreat".

There were 39 girls in 1905, 69 in 1915—and 94 in 1925. In 1920 there were 31 girls in the Upper School, 36 in Middle School and 23 in Lower School: total 90.

A more formal evidence for any school's history lies in the reports of H.M. Inspectors. Every self-respecting independent school after the 1902 Education Act, sooner or later sought "recognition as efficient", a status brought to an end only in 1977—on the grounds that such inspections occupied too much Inspectorate time, and that the schools should find their own ways of certifying their standards. Most independent schools sought "recognition" as soon as possible, but in Ascot's case this did not happen until 1931. Before that, I have to assume that a small school, run by and intimately linked to a community of nuns, was not greatly bothered by what the official world thought. Nor does it seem that the school invited in other distinguished outsiders to give a personal opinion, a practice commonly followed by many important schools even then. It did, however, care about religious education, and in 1924 asked the Portsmouth Diocesan Religious Inspectors, who were priests, to visit and assess the School's teaching. One result was that it joined the Catholic Social Guild which set examinations in this subject. A course of lectures to outline the work required, and a talk from the Jesuit secretary of the Guild led to excellent examination results. The report sent to the school said: "The general level of the papers was high . . . in answering questions on family life, they showed an intelligent and sympathetic understanding of the duties and difficulties of the housewife . . . the more difficult questions dealing with objections of non-Catholics, though outside the scope of the textbooks, were tackled courageously." It is interesting to note that the purpose of St Mary's was seen to be "helping to restore society to the happier state that we all desire." Where did this backwards look take them? In the same issue of the magazine as these quotations appeared there is a high-minded report of a discussion of

"Ideals for Girls". So the discussion went on, and, notice well, not a single word or reference to Home Life had been breathed! We had rung the changes on Sport, Music, Writing, Travel, Slumming, a University Career, even the Teaching of the Poor, but not a word about home! At last, two of the number woke up to the fact that there is something surpassingly beautiful about home-life . . . Surely, our girls have something greater and nobler to do than to visit picture palaces and play games. We are Christians—nay, we are Catholics—and our lives must be worthy of the name.

5

The Headships of Mother Ignatius
and Mother Mercedes, 1921 to 1956,
and a Brief History of Errollston, 1936 to 1970

After Mother Cecilia, the next most memorable nun in Ascot's history was Mother Ignatius Beveridge, headmistress for twenty-seven years, from 1921 to 1949. When I asked her nephew, J. M. Beveridge, whether she was very Irish, he replied emphatically "no".

> She was educated in Ireland at the famous Sacred Heart Convent in Roscrea, County Tipperary—from which she was expelled—and on a visit to England in her 'teens, she was somehow noticed by the IBVM who, I gather, "worked on her" to join them at about the time the Ascot school was starting . . . My sister tells me that she was quite definitely "recruited" by the Order . . . My own recollection of her is of a very English lady.

From 1913 she had been Form Mistress and Mistress of Discipline, and the chief supporter of Mother Cecilia. When I asked in the school magazine that people should write in with their memories and reflections, I received more about Mother Ignatius than anyone else; it has been harder to retrieve memories of other important Sisters. The obituary notice in the School magazine for 1965, recorded her death on 3rd June of that year. She had been, in fact, the most active presence in the school for thirty-five years—to many girls, a more immediate presence than Mother Cecilia. The obituary notice was frank. Her formidable qualities were unmistakeable and unavoidable, and it is clear that many girls came to appreciate her properly only after they had left. She was not, in the ordinary sense, popular, but "a figure of great dignity, able to inspire all by her mere appearance. Many a delinquent quailed at the sweeping entry and well-known (purely rhetorical) question: 'What, may I ask, is the meaning of this?'" This ability to strike quickly and accurately seems to have earned her, surreptitiously, the nickname of "Bomber Command". (The girls were not to know how inaccurate the real Bomber Command could be, and many have expressed great surprise to me about this nickname.) In everyday life, she was either Ig or Ignay, but certainly not to her face.

Erica Kisielewska Dunbar/O'Donnell thinks that Mother Ignatius' most profound influence lay in her phrase for which the pupils, aged 15 or 16, most mocked her: "Self-control and courtesy". She writes

> I cannot think of any happenings in a fairly varied life that would not have been improved had I followed her counsel. I can hear her voice now, and the regular rapid step of her walk and the peculiar swish of her habit as she was about to turn into the Long Passage. Hearing her step, I not only examined my guilty conscience for what I had done, but also for what I was intending to do. In later years I told her this and she was clearly pleased as well as amused.

She records, with great affection, the love and care shewn her, and the significant amount of private tutoring given. "She was notably intelligent and would have made a mark in any field. Certainly, not all children loved her; she was very strict, but for our good." A piece of information to which I have seen no reference elsewhere, is that she was the niece of Sir William Beveridge, the author of the Beveridge Report and the intellectual founder of the Welfare State.

Reminiscences of Mother Ignatius abound: of her pet cure for hiccoughs—making the victim hold tight to a pen-knife and concentrate hard while she held the other end. One much-repeated story tells of an episode at the swimming pool. A child dived in and continued to swim under water. This, to Mother Ignatius, seemed to go on unnecessarily long. Turning to an unknown and astonished bystander, she said commandingly, "Go down at once and tell her to come up." One Old Girl wrote: "I suppose we'll never know, till we join her, just how much we owe to her for the standards formed in our young years. Perhaps, when it is my turn to reach the doors of heaven, a familiar figure, looking so much taller than in reality, will come to look me over and help me through the judgement. May she rest in peace. Amen."

She certainly left her mark, and the memory remains. "She wanted us all to be perfect; she interpreted this ideal with a lack of imagination which inevitably led to an excess of zeal. Everything was either black or white to her, tolerance was a sign of weakness ... indeed there were girls at Ascot who disliked the school because of fear of her." So writes Catherine Devas/Nolan, who was at the school from 1933 to 1940. "On the decision of Mother Ignatius rested the difference of a happy childhood and a wretched one." But, eventually another side of her was found. "My future husband expressed a strong desire to meet Mother Ignatius. Of all odd times, we called in at Ascot on the way back from our honeymoon. She and my husband met with mutual approval. After tea he said suddenly to her, 'Mother Ignatius, you aren't an ogre at all!' She was delighted by his candour. I can see her now, rocking gently backwards and forwards in her chair, overcome with laughter. The mask was down at last." This is the kind of remark a man might get away with to her, and not a woman. Lady Layfield/Harvey adds further to my knowledge of this extraordinary woman, "so worldly-wise and, to give you an example, a great help to my mother in advising her about divorcing my father (both Catholics). She knew all about the problems of sex and marriage. She was such a powerful headmistress, so that pupils either liked her or disliked her."

With great difficulty a photograph of Mother Ignatius, alone, has been found, apparently as she checks girls onto a bus. The photograph lives up to her reputation. Some girls remember her with extraordinary love. She was good at detecting the lonely or the inadequate. Lady Antonia Fraser wrote about her for the *Independent*, in a series called "My Hero". It is the fullest and frankest tribute to her. Lady Antonia's friends thought that she was mad when she told them that she intended to write about Ig in a series devoted to heroines or heroes.

> She was extremely frightening at times—if not downright terrifying . . . her face was notably blanched, even against the whiteness of the wimple which surrounded it; the corners of her mouth turned down sharply and her nose, too, had a downward curve to it, which gave her in profile something of the look of Piero della Francesca's Urbino Duke. The circular black wire spectacles, which concealed her very small sharp eyes were, on the other hand, not particularly ducal; but they were the most menacing aspect of her appearance.

Lady Antonia remembers that Mary Ward was "a great enemy of ignorance", and that that description would go for Mother Ignatius too.

> Not for Ig the kind of lackadaisical education generally thought to be suitable at the time for future Catholic wives and mothers; it was to the glory of God that one should be educated to the top of one's bent, as it were, just as it was to the glory of God that one should execute a Jacobean tapestry cushion without spotting it with the blood of clumsy fingers . . . Professionalism was finally the great lesson of that convent's education under Mother Ignatius' aegis . . . Professional nun, professional teacher, professional wife and mother—even, if you must, professional journalist—but amateurism was not, definitely not, to the greater glory of God. Years later, writing my first Jemima Shore mystery, (*Quiet As A Nun*), which I set in this same convent, I used the character of Mother Ignatius . . . Originally my "Mother Ancilla" was intended to be unsympathetic, authoritarian, worldly and certainly frightening. But she ended up, I found—determinedly

humorous, a perfectionist and a great enemy of ignorance—
being the heroine of the story; as Mother Ignatius has, indeed,
ended up as mine.

Mother Ignatius' family regard this pen portrait as the best of her. In
Lady Antonia's novel, Mother Ancilla is described as someone with
whom "no-one bandied words and stood much chance of emerging
the victor. Especially about Almighty God, someone whose intentions, mysterious as they were to the whole world, were somehow
less mysterious to Mother Ancilla than to the rest of us. In the language of today, one would have referred to Mother Ancilla as having
a hot line to God: or perhaps an open line was the correct term . . .
Mother Ancilla never forgot an adversary." Although "a great
enemy of ignorance", Mother Ignatius was herself not a good
teacher. She failed to detect when pupils could not understand and
frightened them off from asking questions. In the long years of her
headship, no changes were made to the curriculum (except those
caused by a lack of nuns—Lady Antonia also recalls that the Science
laboratory was locked in her time—from 1946 to 1948—because
there was no nun who could teach the subjects). Art was circumscribed by an inability to get beyond religious pictures. Music was
taught, instrumentally and chorally, by Mother Campion Davenport, who seems to have been the only other powerful personality
amongst the Sisters at the time, but little or no attention was given
to listening to records or talking about music. In some ways the real
Mother Ancilla was more important in the girls' eyes, because she
was the Chapel organist and choir mistress. Outside Chapel, there
was little creative aesthetic education, apart from needlework and
dressmaking. Chapel was central in more ways than the simply religious. Here were brought together singing (often to Mother Campion's settings), organ-playing, flower-arrangement, and the most
scrupulous and exacting conduct of every liturgical point. Daily
Mass, Benediction three times a week, and the splendours of Sunday, provided a concentrated sensuous experience for so many girls.
The protocol of Chapel on Sundays was a procession led by

Mother Cecilia and the rest of the choir nuns in order of seniority of profession, followed by the lay Sisters in the same order, followed by the girls in seniority of age. The whole power structure was there. The Chapel was in its original arrangement with benches designed to be comfortable. Catherine Devas/Nolan writes of the atmosphere in the school in those years, recalling especially

> the high point of the Summer term, the Feast of Corpus Christi. I vividly remember the pale banners carried in procession, the sturdy gardeners in white surplices bearing the canopy, the little girls strewing petals. Sister Barbara would bring down our white veils from the attic; they were of thick tulle and smelled heavily of incense . . . The altar was banked high with white flowers; the aroma of lilies and incense was intoxicating. When Sister Barbara sang Panis Angelicus it was our apotheosis. What had we to fear from death when the path to heaven was so straight? It is easy to dismiss the school of this period, when, as in most convent schools, good behaviour was rated more highly than academic excellence. If there was no sixth form in 1933, it was because our parents did not deem one necessary. We were not expected to make a career, rather to acquire a solid grounding in the tenets of the Catholic Faith . . . Security and happiness in childhood form a cloak which protects from the harsh winds of disappointment which attend us all in later life. That cloak protects me yet.

The Chapel was reordered in 1972 in accordance with the liturgical requirements of Vatican II, by no means to everyone's liking, including Catherine Devas'.

Mother Ignatius was headmistress during the Second World War. This time round, Ascot was not a safe place. It was indeed in an area that would have been fought over if there had been an invasion in 1940—the capture, after the war, of German plans for Operation Sealion shewed where the lines of attack on London from the south coast would have been, and Ascot was amongst them. Even so, the school was not evacuated to some remote part of the island, and the smoke and the inflamed skies above blitzed London could easily be seen. Understandably, quite a few girls were not returned to the school by their parents. On the other hand twelve Sisters and forty girls from the school in Hampstead arrived with little warning, because their previous refuge in Sussex had been even more unsafe. Homes had to be found for them in the neighbourhood as the school was very over-crowded.

It is amazing to find that the Community kept in touch with Rome. For example, in June 1943, when Mussolini was still in power, "Reverend Mother M. Campion returned from Rome where she had been Superior. She was obliged to leave on account of her health . . . the Community in Rome were all well when she left them and the school was prospering." This simple statement raises fascinating questions—how did she travel? Are there other cases of English Religious being allowed back like this from Rome? The abandoning of Rome by German troops in 1944, its declared status as an open city, and finally its capture by Allied troops were causes for great celebration in the school at Ascot.

In that year came the "flying bombs", one of which landed on the Friary School next door, causing much damage but no deaths. The school magazine recorded the expected things: gas-masks practice, taking to the air-raid shelters, the plainness of the rationed food, the maintenance of the blackout curtains which the pupils had made themselves. Casualties were listed with great care: husbands, fathers, fiancés or friends of Old Girls or present girls. Beginning in 1940, lectures in First Aid and Home Nursing were developed into training programmes in nearby hospitals and in 1942, a Girls' Training Corps was formed in the school to concentrate on car maintenance, also with some military drill. Lavinia Watson/French recalls having to pack a little blue suitcase containing day clothes with her torch beside it, before she went to bed. Whenever an air-raid siren was heard, the girls were woken in order to go down to the gym. She remembers gathering up the case and dragging my old eiderdown over my shoulders, having to stagger down from the Top dormitory to the "shelter" in the gym. Sandbags had been piled up outside, and what I can only describe as triple bunks were lined up very close together, covering the whole floor . . . If the "all-clear" sounded early on we climbed up the flight of stairs to the dormitory, otherwise we remained uncomfortably on our piece of canvas until the morning.

Half-term breaks ceased and petrol rationing meant very few saw their parents during term-time. She continues: "The blackout had to be rigorously enforced and I remember how the girls would plead to be allowed to accompany Mother Bridget on her tour round the grounds to check that not a slit of light could be seen from the outside."

The unusual presence of some Italian prisoners-of-war who started to work on the farm caused flutters of excitement as the only man the girls ever saw otherwise was an old friar. "We would gaze from our dormitory window as they (the Italians) brought the Jersey cows to be milked, but I think that was the nearest we ever got to them." Mother Ignatius, with characteristic vigilance, complained on one occasion to a Commanding Officer in the Norwegian Air Force that some of his young pilots were flying low over the games fields and "dipping their wings in recognition of a girl they knew".

In 1940, there is the first evidence of what became usual, an increase in marriages as men were called up or were expecting to be sent abroad. Even so, the strongest remaining impression is that of a sense of life as usual, with full programmes of lectures, film and slide shows, plays and concerts. In 1943, for example, "Miss Arnold gave us a lecture on old instruments, playing on the harpsichord, clavichord, lute and viols", and on Reverend Mother's Feast, on 22nd, "We had ORANGES for breakfast . . . in the afternoon, Reverend Mother visited every form and gave each of them, to their great amazement, a big box of sweets. We are most grateful to Reverend Mother and the Community for saving up all their sweet rations for us." But tragedy was brought nearer with the deaths of loved ones. A senior girl's brother who was serving with a Highland regiment came to visit her. Lavinia Watson/French remembers: "As they walked together up and down the hockey field we all thought how glamorous he looked in his kilted Highland uniform. It was not long after, that news arrived that he had been killed in action." Sometimes Old Girls would come back to school wearing their uniforms (usually as Wrens), which made the younger ones envious and eager to join up themselves. "We couldn't wait to leave . . . but then the war ended and 'emergency service' was no longer the form."

Such reminiscences of the War bring with them many further comments on the nuns. When Mother Cecilia is mentioned, it always seems to be with the same evocation: "A grand old lady, and although we did not see her often, we felt her benign presence . . . When we had air-raids we were brought down to the sand-bagged gym. Reverend Mother always came, bringing not prayer books or rosaries, but playing cards. Anyone who could keep awake was obliged to learn bridge, and no-one dared to let their attention wander to listen for bombs. That, I think, was greatness."—This comes from marvellous recollections sent to us by Cathune Cape/Johnstone. The idiosyncracies of Mother Ignatius are commented on again and again.

> I particularly remember the "+ 10". Looking back at it now, I realise that it was a most unusual form of marking which, sadly, did little to make us think things out for ourselves. We had to go right through the entire Catechism and each girl had to give a word perfect answer to the question which was directed at her. If, at the end, every answer had been correct, ten points were added to the average percentage which had been gained already in all other subjects. It was obviously a great advantage to a girl who could learn parrot fashion, but none to one who had a good average mark for main class work, but was not much good at recital.

Yet again, one is told that people were in awe of Mother Ignatius.

> Mother Ignatius was a terrible disciplinarian. There were long periods of silence and standing in line, and good conduct marks were lost if we did not observe these. But the only sanctions were the loss of marks which, when counted up at the end of the term, meant that one House (either Blues or Whites) had a treat. Those who were naturally conformist did not lose marks, and the more spirited did not care. It was only fear of Mother Ignatius' anger that prevented serious rule-breaking.

Cathune Cape was at St Mary's from 1933 to 1942 and paints a very detailed picture of the school at that time.

> We lived surrounded by nuns, they supervised everything in our lives. We did not feel oppressed by this. On the contrary, we felt very sheltered, loved and cared for. I never remember any girl being unhappy or lonely. Any girl who was less popular or friendless always went or walked or sat with the nun in charge. According to a particular nun's attraction, others would flock round and the lonely one would find herself in the middle of a group . . . As we got older the nuns were always ready to talk over personal problems. Many nuns would come round to special friends to say goodnight. A nun always slept in the Lower School dormitory, and two in a room next to the other dormitories . . . The lay nuns played a big part in our lives, and we could not be unaffected by the devotion with which they went about their mundane tasks. Some we knew well, like Sister Martha who had charge of the front door, and like Sister Philomena who supervised the baths. Others we knew less well, but could hear the chant of the Rosary where our grubby clothes were scrubbed by hand.

This all-embracing care included fetching and carrying the water for washing, and emptying the chamber pots. The beauty of Chapel services and liturgical practice, the superb singing of the choir, trained by Mother Ancilla, combined with the incense and flowers remain stamped on many girls' memories. Marina Warner, who has come to her own distinctive view of religion, nevertheless has expressed a moving appreciation of that aspect of the school's life which inducted her into the Church's liturgical year. Otherwise, it would seem that needlework, taught by Mother Hilda, and dress-making, taught by Mother John, were the strong points.

Free time was, apparently, a cause for grievance. According to Cathune Cape there was not a lot to do. "Many just immersed themselves in a book all the weekend." Things were much better in the Summer, "with the grounds to wander in and the outdoor swimming pool." On religion, she is very frank: daily Mass excused only on health grounds, Benediction twice a week and Evening Prayer in the Chapel. When the Angelus bell rang, everyone stopped where they were to say the prayer. Every class had "Doctrine" every day.

> We were told exactly what to believe, and no discussion or individual thinking was allowed. You had to know but not understand. Great stress was laid on "giving up" and sacrifice, and I hope that some spiritual books that we read have been relegated to the dustbin. But we were encouraged in the spiritual life, and in a sense of right and wrong and the worth of things.

She feels the academic aspect of St Mary's was pretty dismal in the War years.

> We only learnt the humanities, with the exception of chemistry for two years. There was no other science whatsoever. Latin was taught but not Greek, and no other foreign language except French (though there was some individual coaching in German and Italian). Current Affairs was taught only in the Sixth Form, which hardly existed, and we had no idea at all what was going on in the world. The great change came about with the arrival of

Mother Bridget, who entered as a nun the year I entered school. Her sharp mind and broad cultural background enabled her to produce examination results that had never been seen before . . . There was no Upper Sixth, but I suppose it started with me when I stayed on to take the Oxford Entrance in English. I had individual coaching with Mother Bridget and I not only got into Oxford, the first straight from Ascot, but learnt from her very much more than English literature. I could use the Library in so-called leisure hours. It contained no science, politics or economics, only two or three books on philosophy, but plenty of travel, biography and classical English literature. I remember it contained Virginia Woolf's *Orlando*, which puzzled me. I wonder if any of the nuns had read it.

I am sure that often in writing the history of an institution there comes a point when, without conceit, one knows that one has arrived at the essentials and that further information will simply add to but not change the view. I think that this is so with my understanding of Ascot, which in no way diminishes the value of further memories and reflections.

St Mary's so obviously made its mark on its pupils, and there is no escaping the sense of protected happiness—and joyous good humour. Cathune Cape writes: "I would like to comment on the universal sense of good humour displayed by the nuns. As I met nuns from other Orders later in life, I never found this trait so strong as at St Mary's . . . We learnt more from just being with the nuns than from what they tried to teach us . . . I sent my daughter there. Hers is another story." A later generation was going to be more worldly, more travelled, and not so unquestioning; but that too is another story.

Throughout all these years the girls were carefully looked after, watched over, and guided by gentleness. The observance of religious feasts never slackened, and the statement, for the August of 1945, that "it was a gracious act of Our Lady's to send us final peace on the Feast of Her Assumption", was made in simple seriousness. In 1942,

Mother Ignatius was involved in a serious car accident, as recalled by her nephew J. M. Beveridge.

> She and some other Ascot Sisters were returning from Shaftesbury and were in a collision in which Mother Ignatius broke her neck. (I think Sister John Baptist was another victim.) The repairs included "wiring her up" in what the doctors call a cervical spine fixation. This procedure was relatively unknown at the time and resulted from handling war casualties. The job was done by Professor Trueta at the Radcliffe Infirmary and was undoubtedly a "first" for a civilian . . . The injury led to frequent migraines and this coupled with blood pressure led to her eventual retirement to Hampstead.

Her move to become Superior at Hampstead took place in 1949. Recording the end of the rule of Mother Ignatius leaves me with the sense that she was the most unusual and intriguing of all the Sisters who have been headmistress. The *Tablet* had a properly appreciative obituary notice, but the school magazines remained largely preoccupied with the cult of Mother Cecilia.

The transition from Mother Ignatius is a good point to look at the picture of the school painted by its magazine, which first appeared in July 1920, the year before her headship began. School magazines have their limitations; one can smile at well-intentioned bad verse, the interminable records of games results, and, over many years a touching innocence in what interested the girls, and how they wrote about it. Nevertheless, these magazines are the main quarry from which to construct a narrative chronological history of the school from that time. In the Foreword to the first number, Mother Cecilia, then the Headmistress and also the Superior, wrote that she had "high hopes for what the magazine would do to keep each generation of girls in touch with each other."

The contents were controlled by the editor who for a long time was a Sister of the Institute. There was, and there is, an understandable reluctance to put in bad news or critical comment. Any criticism that has occurred has come from "authority" about the girls; in 1977 "it took the Lower 5ths rather longer than usual to develop a fittingly adult attitude to concerts." The record of the activities of the Debating Society was often used for what was no doubt intended to be constructive criticism of girls' performance. Every Holy Day, every Feast, every religious anniversary, every Retreat is chronicled, and the births, deaths and marriages of Old Girls are most devotedly recorded. A change to a larger and more expansive format in 1985 ushered in a more attractive presentation, with more photographs and illustrations, though substantially nothing changed. In 1990 an entirely new layout came in, and an altogether more adventurous policy has been followed since then, with interviews, vignettes, freer comment and many more illustrations, some of which are in colour.

I have not made a general study of school magazines, though I was once asked seriously by a headmaster of Shrewsbury how far one could judge a school by its magazine, but I am quite sure that most of them in the 1920s, 30s and 40s were much the same. At Ascot the general and very strong impression gained already is reinforced, of a tightly-knit community, perfectionist wherever possible, in which religious observances and all school activities were meticulously planned and carried out. Sisters and pupils were very close in their relationships, cleanliness was certainly next to godliness, and punctiliousness in everything was treasured and insisted on. This enclosed and very warm family cared deeply about every girl, not only in her school days, but for all the years, when it was possible, after she left. A few must have rebelled against this and felt that they had had enough—there are one or two publicly well-known names of Old Girls that disappear fairly smartly. In the *Times* for Friday January 14th 1994, Marina Warner (the year's Reith Lecturer) was described as being, at Ascot "a devout Mariolater . . . at 16 she made a vow to imitate the Virgin Mary all her life, receiving a blue ribbon to wear on her breast. Then she discovered sin (i.e. sex) and felt no regret: it was the end of her belief." For her, as for almost all the girls, as far as I can see, the school's overall imprint remains strong.

It is the extraordinary detail by which they lived that may fascinate—and seem almost unbelievable to pupils now. Each girl had to have four dresses, each for different occasions in the week; black veils were worn in chapel on ordinary days and white veils taken out from special storage, smelling fragrantly, for the great occasions. Changes in school uniform were made without much prior notice and to the exasperation of some parents, who found it financially difficult, leading to a murmured but real criticism of Mother Cecilia, that she did not understand and had no idea of the strain imposed. Conformity was insisted upon, and naturally desired by most of the girls; stockings had to be bought at Harrods and one girl's school life was made wretched because hers were bought at Selfridges, marginally cheaper and marginally different in colour and size. The Sisters themselves observed a ritual in clothing, for everyday life, for chapel and for high feast days; only the impossibility of getting a sufficient amount of starch during the Second World War led them to give up the white starched capes.

The unceasing preoccupation with modesty and purity imposed its own rituals: the privacy of the cubicles and washing arrangements, the aversion from bare flesh and, vastly more seriously, the total avoidance of instruction and guidance about puberty and adolescence. When one remembers how strong an emphasis was placed on making a good marriage and having children and being a mother, the absence of any preparation for it must strike anyone examining the school's life in these decades. It might be advanced that Ascot differed in no way from the rest of society at this time, but this would not be true. Though at no point in my own adolescence, either at home or at school were these matters mentioned at all, there was a general adolescent underworld of speculation, prurience—and usually inaccurate information. But at Ascot, I have been told with absolute firmness, the girls, certainly up to the late 1940s, were genuinely innocent and therefore often bewildered by the exhortations from the Sisters, and perhaps even more from visiting Jesuits giving Retreats, to avoid impurity and immodesty in thought, word and deed.

As one example of immodesty, there was the matter of not wearing a vest under the dress in very hot weather. In confession, some girls were hard put to it to think up, even to invent sins of this nature. Those who wished to gain attention by appearing to be repentant sinners found this distinctly hard, stretching the imagination no end. More seriously, some girls were distressed and shocked, and had no-one with whom to discuss their physical developments. The Sisters, for all their care and concern, and the intimacy of small classes, were often remote; as in all convents what went on on the other side of the baize doors was completely unknown to the girls (and for that matter to the lay staff) and led to more speculation.

Even taking account of all this, time and again I have been told of the unsullied happiness of the girls, that school was wonderful and that in later years they could be upset to hear of any changes, even to the arrangement of the estate. It was a self-contained world, where an illicit bicycle ride—to watch the races at Ascot, for example—or going up a forbidden staircase, was a daring excitement. It is not in the least difficult to see that with such an imprint on them, many former pupils were eager, if it could be afforded, to send their own daughters to the school in turn. The magazine for 1959 publishes two photographs of "Old Girls' children at school". Those who are more familiar with the parade of names that had gone through the school will make many more connections than I can, but I notice with interest the young Sarah Boyd-Carpenter, who is interviewed in the 1991 issue as Sarah Hogg, Head of the Prime Minister's Policy Unit in No 10 Downing Street: "The Editor and Caroline Marshall were invited to visit her behind the famous front door, where Caroline plied one of our most successful Old Girls with questions". Sarah Hogg, in turn, sent her daughter, Charlotte, to Ascot.

A telling and almost symbolic element that appears for many years is the annual reporting of "Babies Days", when Old Girls take their babies and small children back to school. In 1951 the first of these days was arranged for June 6th by Mother Mercedes. Mother Ignatius came from Hampstead for the occasion, and after the last reluctant baby had been dragged out of the swimming pool, dried and dressed, it was time for tea. "As we went in, we were met by Reverend Mother Provincial, who must have felt bewildered by the avalanche of children." This contribution is signed by "Mother of Three". There are lots of photographs of the little ones. Or again, in 1958, "Babies Day was as enchanting as ever . . . The proud mothers watch and talk to the nuns, relishing the unusual provision of scores of willing nannies from among the older girls."

The War led to the decision to cease separate publication of news about Old Girls and to put everything into the school magazine. This makes it much easier to follow people through. The magazines are also a record of the life of the IBVM itself at Ascot, not simply of the school. Old Girls entering the Institute, first vows or final profession are proudly noted; moreover those who entered are recorded.

Present-day readers will be interested to note that the magazine for 1950 included that "Congratulations are offered to Madeleine, Christine and Frances Hume, whose brother, George, was ordained at Ampleforth on 23rd July." (In religion, he took the name of Basil.) In 1965, there is a photograph of Mother Ignatius with four Old Girls: Reverend Mother Perpetua, the Provincial; Reverend Mother Ancilla; and Gillian and Wendy Orchard "now in the noviceship". The 1971 issue congratulates "Sister Emmanuel (Gillian Orchard) who took her final vows at Ascot December 1970, and Sister Mark (Wendy Orchard) who took her final vows at Ascot in the presence of His Lordship Derek Worlock, Bishop of Portsmouth, in April 1971."

It was in 1936, in Mother Ignatius' time, that Errollston was opened as a centre for a one-year course in the domestic arts for girls of sixteen and over. This may have indicated an early premonition among the upper-middle classes that they would not go on being served, and would eventually have to help themselves around the home. Some girls came up directly from the school, and others entered from outside, not all of whom were necessarily Catholic. Once established, it became possible for girls from the school to go across the grounds to do their needlework and dressmaking there. A run-down and old-fashioned house was transformed into a bright, comfortable and warm home that was to be remembered with immense affection by so many who were there. It is a very interesting episode in Ascot's history. From 1936 to 1970, in effect, a de-tached or at least semi-detached boarding establishment for girls over sixteen flourished in this house, bought by Mother Cecilia Marshall. They were to study for a National Certificate in Domestic Science and to this were added Apologetics and Literature, taught by Sisters from the main school, who also undertook the tuition of students who needed to re-take some subjects in the School Certifi-cate (later O Level) examination. In the magazine for 1970, "the writer of these notes" recalled how she and her fellow-postulants were sent into the dark, old-fashioned house,

> to turn out the debris of years. None of us will forget the pota-toes growing shoots and leaves under the kitchen sink. Very speedily it became the light, attractive, excellently-equipped house that has provided an admirable training every year for twenty-five girls to prepare them to run their own homes with happy efficiency. The splendid tradition there of Christian home-liness and friendliness, combined with a very high standard of achievement, was built up by Mother Perpetua, and carried on by her successors, Mothers Magdalen and Isabelle. Their many Old Girls remember their year at Errollston with great affection and are lamenting that their daughters cannot have the same happiness.

The magazine, all through the years, gave longer or shorter Erroll-ston Notes. One of the most interesting was for 1953, a personal account of how the year had gone. It was obviously a mixture of hard work to exacting standards, in the kitchens and needlework room: "Needlework was another problem, though whether after all the pastry, cooking chocolate and rich food, not to mention the large quantity of potatoes which we devoured during the year, we shall ever be able to get into those 'little bits of nothing', no-one knows as yet." All this was mixed with cultural visits to theatres, art galleries and, indeed, visits abroad." The theory paper (in Domestic Science) took place on the 29th of June, SS Peter and Paul, and the day before was spent in a Retreat given by Father Crompton S.J. . . . practical tests started on the 7th of July." Every now and then girls came over from the main school for Domestic Science lessons, obviously not provided in the ordinary course of things there.

The English Province of the IBVM published a pamphlet in October 1992, for internal circulation, devoted entirely to recollections of Errollston. One of the first five students, Patricia Paterson/Cardwell, recalled the happy early days. She is "eternally grateful for having been taught how to iron a man's shirt. I remember that a shirt had to be borrowed from the school handyman for us to practise on . . . We all had bicycles and used to cycle to Fort Belvedere and watch all the comings and goings, as it was the time of the Abdication." A much longer essay by Sister Magdalen Ingram and Sister Isabelle McIrvine, describes all the years from 1936 to 1970. Errollston's full capacity was for twenty-four students, all boarders, following a year's course from October to July. The week was spent on cookery, laundry, housecraft and dressmaking in the morning. Afternoons were free except for extra subjects, which varied for each individual and were not compulsory. The daily running of the house was carried out almost entirely by the students on a weekly rota, even answering the doorbells and telephone. At 6.30 pm the Cooks of the Day prepared supper. There was no uniform "except each student inevitably arrived wearing a tweed skirt and twin set . . . At first no make-up of any kind was allowed especially lipstick, but by the early 1940s most seventeen- and eighteen-year-olds felt they were going out at weekends without faces . . . fortunately the ban was lifted." The essay describes what was regarded by so many as a very happy community, which changed from being no more than a finishing school into a place of serious work, so serious that girls there were exempted from National Service during the War. After the War, Errollston meant freedom from school discipline.

> Home clothes! As I and my friends from St Mary's Ascot con-signed our tunics and ties to oblivion, girls from Shaftesbury and other schools were also heading for Errollston and freedom. Unheard-of privileges awaited us . . . for the first time we were treated as grown-ups and it was a heady experience . . . There were other things to be learnt at Errollston however. As we all stood respectfully watching a bed-making demonstration, Sister Magdalen bent her serene gaze upon us and said, 'Remember, you sleep between the right side of the sheets.' A friend and I exchanged anxious glances, wondering whether there were something morally wrong about the other side of the sheet.

So writes Fay Angoy/Hall. This delightful collection of essays ends with one by Sister Agatha Leach entitled 'Gravy was the reason why my family chose to send me to Errollston'.

> It was my mother's inability to make it satisfactorily that focused their choice. Discipline and the nuns' ability to impose it on a wayward sixteen-year-old confirmed my mother's choice. No-one was concerned about Catholicism but it was that which occupied my thoughts and time until it 'took', and I was removed from further contamination six months after arriving. There was not only Catholicism to contend with, but holiness as well.

So this charming essay continues, describing how she returned to acquire a cookery certificate, then as a teacher and finally as a fully professed IBVM Sister up to the closing of Errollston. "By then, I had learnt the Jesuit dictum of finding God in all things, even if the catalyst in my case had been gravy."

By 1970, the pressure of applications for places was so great that "the situation in the school was becoming impossible: over a hundred applications, chiefly from Old Girls or parents with children in the school, for twenty-five places this term. Something drastic had to be done, and so Errollston has become an annexe to the school." It made possible an increase in total numbers and correspondingly in the development of a new and academic Sixth Form.

Mother Ignatius was succeeded by Mother Mercedes Lawler (one of the two sisters who "blew in from Ireland"; the other sister was Mother Perpetua, who succeeded Mother Cecilia as Provincial). She was headmistress from 1949 to 1956. It has not been easy to find out much about her. Nothing is said about her in the magazine until her death on January 31st 1989, a good example of how the official record deals with Sisters in the IBVM. She was not a scholar, nor of a scholarly cast of mind, but she had a delight in personalities. She was widely read, and assumed without any doubt that all the girls would be as interested in her subject as she was. Above everything else she loved teaching History; she also taught some Latin. To be interested in History was, for her, simply a part of being Catholic, and she carried many girls along in her enthusiasm. Antonia Fraser happily acknowledges her debt to Mother Mercedes, leaving with a State Scholarship (one of the two awarded in that year, 1948, for the first time in the school's life) to read History at Oxford. Mother Mercedes' teaching method, as indeed was the case with all the other nuns, was straightforwardly didactic; new ideas on teaching made no appearance, there were few historical atlases or maps, but textbooks were always in good condition. Because there was no proper Sixth Form, individual girls of promise were coached for particular purposes, and took the Higher School Certificate Examination after one year. This may explain why so little attention was given to building up a library capable of supporting scholarship. It is puzzling that so little is recorded of her headship, and few reminiscences of her have reached me. It is said that she governed with a quiet but firm discipline, and did much to inculcate a spirit of courtesy and consideration. She was, according to Lady Layfield/Harvey, "diminutive, pretty with small features and laughing eyes; gentle and shy but a wonderful teacher who made everything interesting and fun". Her health was precarious, and many felt that she should never have been given the headship. The strains on her increased her attacks of cardiac asthma, and brought Mother Cecilia to the decision to relieve her of her responsibilities. This elusive personality, coming between dominating women, seems to have been destined to be over-shadowed. Even as she laid down office, the school was preoccupied with the celebrations of Reverend Mother Provincial's Diamond Jubilee. The school magazine put it this way:

> The greatest joys often seem to have their cross. The Old Girls' celebration of the Diamond Jubilee was marred by the sudden serious illness of Mother Mercedes, who received the Last Sacraments on the eve of April 29th (1956), and had to be taken to Windsor Hospital. Although she made a wonderful recovery, she was not, unhappily for all of us, allowed to do any work throughout the Summer Term. She has now been obliged to lay down the office of headmistress, which is a matter of universal regret.

Mother Bridget has always said that she was expecting to take over the headship because she had been standing in for Mother Mercedes for some time.

In 1931, came the first Inspection of the school. Whitehall never respected religious nomenclature; the headmistress is listed as Miss G. M. Beveridge. The next full Inspection fell during the November of 1953, when Mother Mercedes Lawler was headmistress. This means that we have an official account and assessment by outsiders of the educational provision as it stood in their times. (There was a third Inspection at some time during the 1960s when Sister Bridget was headmistress. She is innocently and charmingly vague about it, thinks it was conducted by Lady Helen Asquith, and seems to remember that the Report was left in the third drawer on the right of her desk when she left to go to Cambridge.) The rules by which

H.M. Inspectors operated required the recording of what was heard and seen; no contextual information, no quasi-sociological perceptions were allowed. The task was to inspect teaching but not teachers. Reports were confidential to those responsible for the school and only appropriate parts of the text were shewn to the teaching staff or parents. In 1931, secondary independent and maintained grammar schools were the responsibility of a small group of H.M. Inspectors whose work lay entirely in this field. By 1953, much of the 1944 Education Act had been implemented, and the team was drawn from a wider field. Always the accepted practice was to talk about far more than what was written, and not to write what had not been talked about. At St Mary's, all that this meant was that the Reports were seen by a closed group—the Provincial, the Superior and the Headmistress.

The Report of 1931 began by noting that there were 122 pupils, all boarders, which were as many as could conveniently be accommodated. The normal age for admission was eight, and it would seem that children were admitted at all ages from nine to fifteen, and left at all ages from eleven to eighteen. Some girls took the Oxford School Certificate Examination, and a few stayed on for some months or a year for work to individual timetables. Between 1928 and 1931, seven girls had gone to a university and twenty-two to other places of higher education. More than forty members of the IBVM. lived in the Community at that time. For school purposes there were eight classrooms, a laboratory, an art room, a gymnasium, hall, library, music room, needlework room and cookery room. There were seven dormitories of which the smallest held four and the largest nineteen; there was also a number of private rooms, fourteen single, thirteen double and two triple. The library was adequate for the type of teaching. Thirteen members of the Institute taught, with a visiting Physical Training mistress and eight visiting teachers of music, art and elocution. Of the Sisters, only three were graduates, and there was no-one with a degree in either Mathematics or Science. Everyone taught more than one subject, making up in patience and zeal for the lack of the "vigorous attack of the trained specialist", but the Inspectors also thought that the girls could, and should, do more for themselves.

Organisation was simple: eight successive forms, with annual promotions. English, History, Geography, Arithmetic and Nature Study began in the lowest form, with a little French. Algebra and Geometry were added in the next form, and Latin and Science a year after that. This whole cluster of subjects was then followed for two years, after which there was considerable freedom in dropping subjects. Even though languages were optional extras, quite a lot of girls passed the Oxford Examination in as many as five foreign languages.

Subjects were reported on one by one. English and History were acceptable, but suffered much from being taught by a number of teachers. Geography was not in very good form, dropped as soon as it could be—"The standard of work was unsatisfactory throughout the school". German was taught "by a native of Germany, who is also concerned with the teaching of needlework. The lessons are not regular form work, and do not appear on the timetable." (Sixteen years later, Antonia Fraser struggled with a growing sense of failure to embroider a cushion cover, but loved learning German at the same time with "Mutter Hilda".) Latin was acceptable, Mathematics seems to have had far too many teachers, including the headmistress, "who though not academically qualified is an experienced teacher". The teaching was patient if not exciting. Science was clearly not a strong point in the school, the teacher being not academically qualified, and also inexperienced and diffident. There was a conspicuous lack of practical work throughout the Sciences, and far too much vague repetition of back work. A very quaint custom prevailed of destroying all the pupils' notebooks at the end of the Summer Term.

Art became a voluntary subject in the upper forms, and there was much good work. Music came out well, with a lot of instrumental work and much practice in plainsong and unaccompanied part singing (no doubt for use in Chapel). Two- thirds of the girls learnt the piano, but no-one learnt the organ in spite of having a splendid instrument in the Chapel. And so the Report went on, noting the healthy and happy life of the girls. The school was granted Recognition and praised for doing valuable work.

The Inspection of 1953 was an altogether more detailed affair. It referred to the history of the Institute, and to the previous Inspection. It noted that since then, Errollston had been bought and made into a separate Domestic Science school; Gilmuire, bought in 1947, was being used both for boarding and teaching, so enabling two classrooms in the main building to be converted into very pleasant common rooms for the Sixth and Fifth Forms. The usual pattern of reporting was followed, but with a clear preoccupation with a new development that was facing the school with certain difficulties, namely the beginnings of a recognisable proper academic Sixth Form. The problem was that,

> Hitherto, for many, perhaps the majority of the parents who use this school the former School Certificate [the newly entitled General Certificate of Education had just come in] has represented the summit of their academic ambition. Once that has been achieved they want their daughters to complete their education either by a year abroad, or by a year's Domestic Science course, or by both, and they do not willingly contemplate a year, still less two years, in the Sixth Form. By the device of preparing girls for Advanced Level papers in one year the School has been successful in inducing a large proportion to stay for a year in the Lower Sixth. Fourteen stayed on into the Upper Sixth, but only four of them completed a whole year.

All this was seen as making it difficult for the school to contribute fully to the intellectual development of the really able girls. These matters were returned to in the conclusions of the Report.

The library was found to be dignified, austere, well-furnished but not a place in which books could be enjoyed. Five thousand books were kept in cupboards of which only the upper sections had glass-fronted doors. The sections for subjects varied considerably in the number, the range and the usefulness of books in them. The section on Mathematics was almost non-existent. Only the Upper Fifth and Sixth Forms were allowed to work in the library and to borrow books freely. The library was less and less suited to the way the school was developing. (More than one Old Girl has felt that the library did not match the school at this period.)

Mother Mercedes not only ran the school as headmistress, but also taught all the senior work in History, some Mathematics and was Sixth Form Mistress. Thirteen out of the eighteen teachers were Sisters of the Institute; the other five were part-time. The practice of teaching more than one subject continued to be normal, resulting on the whole in competent rather than scholarly teaching. Many of the Sisters were seriously over-worked, but their vitality and infectious gaiety earned them much praise.

There follow the subject reports. "Little need be said about the English of this school. The girls come with great advantages and the school develops them." Seventeen girls were reading the subject in the Sixth Form and benefitting enormously from the teaching of a Sister who had taken a First Class Honours Degree in French and English. The infectious enthusiasm of Mother Mercedes as a History teacher was appreciated, but it was commented that in the main school, too much was done for the girls. Geography was a bit better than last time. The Sister-in-charge was trying hard but, "it is not easy for her at her time of life to alter her methods, or to attend courses". Latin was diligently studied with much effort put into oral work, which imposed a considerable strain on the teacher. Some girls learned Greek outside the timetable, and made a success of it.

French was a mixed bag. "The Mistress has so much to give that it seems the greatest pity that she must press on with preparation for examination answers, and that there is so little time for girls to make their own discoveries." Spanish, German and Italian were also taught, Spanish unsuccessfully by a young Spanish girl with "little understanding of how to teach and with an imperfect command of English". Mathematics was in good shape. Science was limited, not least by the possession of one laboratory only. Art and Craft flourished but, "making Art an extra for senior girls is out of keeping with modern educational practice". Housecraft and needlework were showered with praise. Skilled members of the Institute taught them, and Errollston was across the way. The highest standards were insisted upon. For the only time in either Report, the Lay Sisters are mentioned, "who play an important though unobtrusive part in helping to keep the wheels oiled and smoothly running". Errollston was a venture of which the Community should be proud.

There is a long report on Music, flourishing in choral work, and with three weekly periods for almost all Forms in the School. "It is pleasing and appropriate to find that it is in their Chapel services that the girls receive their fullest musical experiences. The choice of music and manner of performance, both by choir and congregation, are entirely worthy of the beauty of the setting." The instrumental side of the School also received great praise.

After all this, Physical Education, which was obviously much enjoyed, with plenty of provision for hockey, tennis, netball and, of course, the open-air swimming pool that Mother Cecilia Marshall had had built, comes as a sort of after-thought, though I do not suppose that this was intended.

It makes for good reading, a good Report on a school in which the girls led "an extremely full and happy life". They heard Mass every morning, and recited the Rosary or attended Benediction each evening. There seems to have been remarkably little misbehaviour, and there is no mention of forms of punishment—though one, I believe, was to sit for a stated time in the Book Room. Perhaps it was the last age of innocence.

6

The Headship of Mother Bridget: 1956 to 1976

Mother Bridget has been introduced already, as the outstandingly inspiring young teacher of English, remembered by a number of Old Girls, and praised for her work in the Report of 1953. The uncertain health of Mother Mercedes had already prepared her for the succession. When it came, it had the inevitability of the unavoidable. She writes

> Mother Cecilia appointed me in a few simple words: "There's no-one else, my dear. You'll have to carry on." With such a *faute de mieux* introduction I was kept well in my place. Little did either of us know that it was to be a twenty-year assignment. About fifteen years later, I was very ill with blood poisoning. Not feeling quite myself, I asked Mother Perpetua, who followed Mother Cecilia as Provincial, if I could stop being headmistress, but the answer was clear: "Go on." I suppose my term of office was thus marked by its beginning and ending: no fuss, no questioning. You just went on for better, for worse.

The twenty years of this headship, which included the Sixties, now so much reminisced about, saw considerable changes in the school. Entry began to be broadened and numbers increased. A two-year sixth form was developed, and entry to Oxford and Cambridge became a more ordinary conclusion to school life. In 1956 two university entrants were recorded; in 1976 there were eleven.

> My great objective was to build up the Sixth Form. In 1956 there were twelve girls, and twenty years later there were forty-six. I

must confess [writes Sister Bridget] that I expedited the increase by jumping the very clever pupils up the school a year ahead to make sure that they got two years in the Sixth Form. (This is known as fast-streaming.) It was not, I admit, the best method educationally, as some of my long-suffering Community staff pointed out, but it worked for a time without any apparent detriment to the pupils' brains. The Sciences gained an unexpected boost when John Boyd-Carpenter expressed a desire for his daughter Sarah to study them at Advanced Level. As he was an influential member of the Cabinet and his wife was a very clever Old Girl, the powers-that-were grew more amenable to my pleas for another laboratory, and so one was made possible. Sarah eventually took Advanced Level English, French, Italian, Pure Mathematics and Applied Mathematics. And so parents became more convinced of the value of a two-year Sixth Form. I remember a would-be member of the Sixth lamenting bitterly that she was not really A Level material because she was so often asked at parties, by somewhat incredulous people, whether it was true that she was going to take A Levels. The days of secretarial, domestic, and finishing courses were over.

So many of the Old Girls who are now prominent in national life, or have made their mark in service to the school, were pupils during these years. Mother Bridget is remembered for unceasing hard work, her magisterially autocratic ways, and her determination to continue teaching English, where she is universally acknowledged to have been idiosyncratic and outstanding. Her defence is that she herself was under orders from both the Provincial and the Superior, who were resident in the same house, and that she was never consulted about money, fees, or general policy. (There are some people who say that she told them what to tell her.) There was, in fact, no consultation about anything. Admission to the school itself was not entirely in her control. Whether she chose, or whether her Superiors did, this could be decidedly quixotic, even unpredictable. Mother Bridget worked from the earliest morning to the latest night, with a secretary, but no other office staff and no bursar. The secretary, Mother John Baptist, by controlling the post, the telephone and the diary, exercised considerable influence. Decisions about new buildings or equipment were taken by Mother Bridget's Superiors, if money were available. On one occasion, she was asked to choose, for example, between a gymnasium and a concert hall; both could not be afforded. She chose the gymnasium.

In these years a Community of more than sixty Sisters lived in a completely separate world from everyone else on the estate. It did not occur to them to open up discussion about issues affecting the school. The close handling of money was eventually to bring major problems, but these were not evident in the years of Mother Bridget's headship. In 1961, the first full-time lay member of staff was appointed, and Mlle Arlette Kalflèche is still happily teaching French. Her salary and terms of appointment were fixed without much reference to national practice, and the same procedure was followed in the coming years as more lay staff were appointed, each on individual terms, quite often built around their private, or domestic, or recreational circumstances—that, for example, Thursday was golf day.

In no sense does Sister Bridget, for she is no longer Mother, think that she was an educational pioneer at the frontiers of curriculum development. These were, after all, the years of the rise (and fall) of the Schools Council, when publications on every aspect of the primary and secondary curriculum came flooding out. In 1974, I was commissioned to organise many of my colleagues in the Inspectorate to re-examine the curriculum for the compulsory years of schooling in order to answer two questions:

1. If pupils are required to be at school for eleven years, what should be seen as necessary knowledge and necessary experience for all?

2. If pupils were to experience such a newly-thought-out curriculum, by what means would their progress and achievement be measured accurately?

The processes that began as a result of all these activities led to discussion and argument that has increased in volume and scope, and emotional tension, in all the years since. Amongst other things, the National Curriculum, Records of Achievement, and Pupil Profiling, and much else, have grown from these arguments and are now fixed in the national system. In the year that Sister Bridget gave up the headship (and went to be Superior at Cambridge), James Callaghan gave at Oxford the first speech entirely about education ever to be given by a British Prime Minister.

At Ascot, the curriculum was still determined largely by the talents of the Sisters put at the headmistress' service, or as I have shewn, as a result of parental pressure. There was nothing particularly unusual about this. Girls' independent schools in these years were much the same, giving most attention to the Arts subjects, and only slowly recognising that the Sciences must become an essential part of education. Sister Bridget writes

The Old Girls' Association grew and prospered. There were far more opportunities for organised meetings then than now. Reunions at Ascot, days of recollection, a Holy Week Retreat when possible, a Summer "Babies' Day", luncheons in London were all features of my time. The last recorded Retreat was in 1983. Parents' visits to the school were more and more frequent, though there were still too few who followed up their children's progress. My memories, I regret to say, are more of mothers complaining about school uniform than about their lessons. Prospective parents, whose daughters we had been unable to take into the school, could be very difficult. I remember one father who threatened to blacken my name throughout the City, which would not, I thought, trouble the City over much. Another told me that his uncle, a Bishop, would sit up in his coffin and howl had he known of his great-niece's rejection. Yet a third wrote to the Cardinal and to the Mother General in Rome, but their answers were extremely reassuring. I think the only parent who made me feel really nervous was Evelyn Waugh. I was sent to take him and his wife around the school before I was headmistress. Having helped

himself to a button-hole from Sister John's lovely floral arrangement in the parlour, he looked just like the cat who had stolen the
cream . . . His postcards were unparalleled for brevity and wit.
The only one that comes to my mind was his reply to a request for
permission to have the school hairdresser cut his daughter's hair:
"You may cut my daughter's hair as short and as frequently as you
wish, providing you do not lengthen the school holidays."

Sister Bridget is particularly interesting and pointed about religious observances and practices as they varied through the years.

Just before she died, Mother Cecilia said to me: "Let Benediction
go, let Rosary go, but try to keep the daily Mass". I was also
encouraged by Abbot Basil Hume of Ampleforth saying to me:
"Yes, I try to hang on to week-day Mass. I would rather people
thought that I was too keen on the Mass than thinking I did not
feel it mattered very much." I also remember Abbot Passmore of
Downside saying to me: "Don't worry about buildings and
equipment. Good food, good teaching and the Faith, that's what
matters."

She records that the Corpus Christi procession came to an end
just after she left in 1976. She recalls the many outstanding retreat-
givers, mainly eminent Jesuits but also Mgr Ronald Knox. "Retreats
for the whole school, excluding the three youngest forms, were serious and lengthy, lasting three full days, more or less in silence. The
girls of that period could take quite easily what must seem intoler-
able strictness to their successors. They did not live in a world hum-
ming with noise and talk, or against a background of music, if you
can call it that." She remembers the flourishing religious societies,
the personal devotions: "There was a tradition of silence and recollection which would be impossible to recapture." Sister Bridget con-
cludes her memories by talking about the staff in her time, nearly all
members of the Community, not forgetting the hard-working lay
Sisters.

The Community formed a wonderful team and contained some first-rate teachers, amongst them Sister Emmanuel Mulcahy, who taught History, Geography ("We will now run through the tropical forests") and Current Topics. She was a poetry lover like myself, and could quote reams unhesitatingly . . . In those days we were all form mistresses. Not only did one teach one's subject, sometimes up to forty or more periods a week, one had charge of a form and took turns to take study supervisions, meal times, putting children to bed. There was no doubt about it, it was very exacting, but one knew one's children through and through . . . When I began as headmistress, twelve at least of the Community were full-time teachers; when I retired in 1976 there were barely half a dozen.

Mlle Arlette Kalflèche has been willing to talk and to write about her own thirty-two years of teaching in the school. She remembers so clearly that other world to which the tiled passage beyond the chapel led. Every teaching Sister could be summoned by a personal ring of bells if the headmistress or the Superior wished. The lay staff had no part in the pastoral care of the children: no duties of any kind, just teaching. The lay staff wrote pupils' reports in pencil, which were then taken away and "processed" by the nuns—inked over, erased, altered: the lay teachers never saw the results.

We did not know any parents. We were not encouraged to attend the annual Prize-Giving Day—then the Library was transformed into a select dining-room, with all the silver and porcelain out . . . The school farm was wonderful but in the end just did not pay—Sister Agatha used to say when we had a glass of milk: "Remember, you are drinking gold". Nothing could be done without Sister Bridget's approval—it was a very centralised regime—an autocracy really—which we accepted because the autocrat was no ordinary person.

She says that they stayed because the school was a beautifully- run and happy place; they taught within limits, but they were most courteously looked after—taking their meals in a separate room, waited on by Lay Sisters, the table presided over by Miss Frith, the resident friend of Mother Cecilia. There was a list, pinned in the secretary's office of "visiting staff", as they were all regarded; it was to include the first-ever Deputy Head, a lay person.

Sister Bridget left for Cambridge in 1976. Writing to me she said, "It may seem a little strange to you, but I was so determined to put the next objectives in my life first, that is Superiorship at Cambridge for six years and at Hampstead for three, that quite deliberately my memory was not allowed to hark back to Ascot. When I did return, the whole system had changed."

It is possible to see the years 1920 to 1976 as a unit of time, a period of history at St Mary's, where there were more or less unchanging features in the school's life. Already it has been remarked often that they seem to have been years of simple happiness and a sort of preserved innocence. The one thing that I have been told insistently by many Old Girls is that they were happy at school. I want to emphasise this, because writers of school histories can be accused of "white-washing", of not knowing the "real school", even of "propagating a myth". I can go only on what I have been told orally or in writing. I do know that no adult can claim truly to know the whole truth about any educational institution in which they work, and they are deceiving themselves greatly if they think otherwise. However, it still remains that I have been told insistently of the happiness of the girls in these years.

Though there were visiting lecturers and organised outside visits, "the world" was kept at arm's length. Because teaching Sisters and Lay Sisters worked for nothing, fees could be kept low, and there was no sense of proper budgeting or housekeeping. The school kept itself full and steadily increased in numbers without any need for public advertisement. That these were the "roaring twenties", that the great Slump began with the Wall Street Crash on October 29th 1929, leading to mounting unemployment—in June 1931, it was

2,700,000—and that for most of the Thirties, Depression, the Dole Queue and the Means Test cast the darkest shadows over national life, these were not much noticed at Ascot, if the school magazine is anything to go by. True enough, J. B. Priestley, in his *English Journey* in 1933, noticed that there were two Englands, North and South (so, I believe, had Mrs Gaskell), and that the South was much less affected by the Slump—an experience gained also by the Jarrow Hunger Marchers. Parents wanted good Catholic schooling for daughters who would make good marriages. Quite a number, in fact, entered the IBVM, and some entered other Orders. The Magazine can be used randomly to illustrate this; in 1920 Germaine Gilbert entered the Novitiate, in 1928 Consuela Littlehales took her first vows; moving on, one notices that Sister Benedict (now Sister Helen Butterworth) received the Habit in April 1944, that Moylena North (now Sister Francis, erstwhile Provincial and now Superior in Cambridge), entered the Novitiate in October 1947, and that Isabella McIrvine made her Final Profession as Mother Isabelle in 1949. It seemed natural and normal for girls to enter the Institute. Its life and theirs were interlocked.

It is easy to understand how and why the Community was naturally conservative. It was hierarchical; each Sister was ranked in order of year of Profession, but the teaching Sisters always took precedence over the Lay. I am sure that the taking of "names in religion" gave a dignity and separateness; Mother M. Mercedes Lawler is rather more impressive than Miss Eileen Lawler, and Mother M. Ignatius more than Miss G. M. Beveridge, as the Board of Education addressed her. The magazine rightly valued and respected the Marthas, the Lay Sisters. On September 5th 1934, Sister Crescentia Drexel, one of the founding members in 1885, celebrated her golden Jubilee. "She still controls the furnace, the laundry and the chickens." When she died in November 1948, it was written that

she came to England from Germany as a Postulant and received the Habit in 1884. All the Convent's oldest friends and many of the pupils will miss her holy old face which used to light up with such a beaming welcome for them. She was busy with the laundry work and the chickens until very near the end of her devoted life, and with advancing years lived more and more in the Courts of Heaven, until her conversations with God and His Saints became quite audible.

Four years earlier, it was recorded that Sister Ludmilla died, who had entered the Institute at Eichstatt in 1895. "She was very hardworking and most efficient, most closely associated with the kitchen garden." Sister Margaret, "who had cooked for the school for nearly thirty years", died in 1969. Coming forward into recent years, it tells us that in 1984 Sister Philomena and Sister Georgina went into retirement. "Sister Philomena's watchful guardianship of the bath towels will be memorable to many generations, but perhaps not so many know that every holiday throughout the sixty-two years she was at Ascot, she was out with her paint brush touching up the kick marks left on doors and walls by the generations who have trod none too lightly these corridors." As for Sister Georgina, "with her blue apron, her mop and friendly solicitude, she became part of the timelessness of Ascot—or so it seemed. However, since the nuns gave up the daily cleaning of the whole school, her mopping of the entire premises had to be confined to Saturdays and Sundays. Sister Georgina felt it as the passing of an era." And so it was.

Another watershed had been reached in 1960. The magazine for 1961 records the death of Reverend Mother Provincial, Cecilia Marshall on October 10th 1960. "It would be impossible to gauge the extent of all she did for Ascot, and precisely because she accomplished so much, her spirit cannot be lost. It is enshrined in stone, moulded in characters, and scattered far and wide in the countless souls she trained and loved." The Requiem Mass for her was sung on October 13th 1960 by Archbishop John Henry King, "and a galaxy of the great and good in the Church came to her funeral. Cardinal Godfrey celebrated a Requiem Mass for her at Westminster Cathedral on October 22nd. A Bishop of Portsmouth had clothed her, and the Archbishop-Bishop of Portsmouth gave her the last blessing just before she died." I have not been able to find much information about the relationship between the convert Cecilia Marshall and the down-to-earth, memorable champion and scholar of recusant England, John Henry King, who to this day is a sort of patronal figure of the Portsmouth diocese. Certainly they respected each other as individuals, and all high ecclesiastics were received courteously in the Parlour; but her natural instinct and sympathy were always with the Jesuits. She would have been proud to have been called a Jesuitess.

When Sarah Hogg was interviewed in 1991, she was asked whether there was anything she particularly remembered about her schooldays. She replied

The moment that impacted on me most was when Reverend Mother Cecilia died. She was beautifully laid out with candles and flowers and we all had to walk past and pay our last respects. As you can imagine, we were all nervous about this activity—I had never seen a dead body before—but I can remember understanding then the very important lesson about the passing of the spirit when a person is dead. [She continued that she saw this memory as an important one because it reinforced her sense of the school as a community.] The point about the community as it was then is that you had the feeling of being somewhere where people's lives were going on—the continuum of their lives. They were not just people who came in, dealt with a lot of tiresome adolescents and then withdrew; they were there right through and you had the living reminders of the later stages of life all around you.

Not all the teaching Sisters were equally talented, but all were devoted, by and large each carrying out a spread of duties that, when replaced by lay staff, would require two people. No-one seems to have been more outstanding than Mother M. Campion Davenport. Hers was a late vocation, entering the IBVM in 1924,

with a considerable career in music already achieved. She was a concert pianist who had been taught by Schumann's daughter. She was
tall and powerful—after all she played the Liszt B Minor Sonata
when she was nearly eighty. Because she thought that the repertoire
of sacred music within the performance of girls was limited, she
began to compose for her choir at Ascot. The very considerable corpus of her work, neglected in more recent years, is now being
revived and performed with great skill. Her teaching life was much
interrupted by duties in Rome; from 1947 to 1953 she was Superior
of the House there, and assistant to the Mother General. Before she
went, she taught the young Antonia Pakenham the piano, with no
success. Surprisingly, though so much choral and instrumental
work went on, little seems to have been done in music appreciation
for the girls in any serious sense.

Until the 1960s, a Community numbering sixty-five and over lived
within the same house as the girls—Provincial, Superior and Headmistress all in the building. The magazine gives a continuous
impression of the centrality of religion. Piety was prominent in
ways that might make some pupils self-conscious now, but it was
not so then. The Sodality of the Children of Mary was very active,
and its affairs reported in detail: Retreats, Masses, admissions of
beginners, charitable activities—in 1925, £5. 12s 6d was sent to "buy"
fifty-four Chinese babies, and more money in 1927. Its members
were exhorted to recognise the "surpassing beauty of home-life", as
against the lures of ambition and careers for women. They sent
Holy medals to Rome to be blessed. The Franciscans in the neigh-
bouring parish—until their withdrawal in 1980—were the Mass
priests and Confessors, but everything else to do with religion was
substantially speaking in the hands of the Sisters. Though the association with the Franciscans was valued, it was to the Jesuits that the
school and the Sodality turned for the truly important occasions,
such as Retreats.

One has to suppose that the members of the Sodality were the
more religiously inclined; though numbers varied, and at times
were quite high, it was always, understandably, a minority of the

school. To refer to Antonia Pakenham again, she recalls being refused admission to the Sodality because she was too independent. She took this as a compliment. The importance of the Sodality was always there. In 1965 "there were thirty-five Children of Mary, meeting on Thursday evenings, but also in special groups every night to practise reading the Introit, Gradual, Offertory and Communion prayers for the next day's Mass." In later years they took on much more challenging tasks, in 1970 helping to instruct thirty children from sixteen Catholic families in the neighbourhood. These were girls, but they also took on boys from Heatherdown and Sunningdale, local prep schools. "Some of their circumstances are very difficult, for instance, some have never been to Mass, or one parent is very much against the instruction. They range from the age of four to fourteen." In 1971 the Sodality gave a party for all the children they instructed who belonged to the parish but were not at Catholic schools. In 1978 the name was changed to the Christian Life Movement because the aims and objectives of Vatican II were being taken seriously, and there was much more direct reference to the Spiritual Exercises of St Ignatius. This is important, because Sister Mark says that in all her time as a pupil at St Mary's, no significant notice was taken of St Ignatius. "In the Christian Life Movement, we find the traditions of the Sodality renewed and interpreted in the spirit of the Council, and we look forward to making contact with sister groups in the Autumn."

Authority was not only respected but accepted unreservedly, not least ecclesiastical authority. The magazine used a particular kind of prose: "We had a glimpse of His Eminence Cardinal Godfrey . . . with fatherly and patient kindness he allowed each child in the school to kiss his ring before he got into his car, an impressive sight in his Cardinal's robes." (This shy, withdrawn Liverpudlian conservative seems to have had a great affection for Ascot. The magazine notes how many times he stayed there, as Apostolic Delegate, Archbishop of Liverpool and Cardinal at Westminster. He would be greatly fussed over.) When Cardinal Hume visited for confirmation in 1992 he would, I think, have been surprised and embarrassed if the pupils, all three hundred and forty of them, had lined up to kiss his ring.

Respect for authority and an habitual sense of loyalty made the Sisters and the girls at Ascot as devoted to the monarchy as were almost all Catholics. Right back in those first jottings describing the life of the school in the early days, mention was made of lining up the girls at the edge of the estate to watch Queen Victoria go by, who was graciously pleased to bow to them. The school marked every Royal occasion, joyful or sad, most carefully. This Royal marriage, that Royal death, a Coronation, all were made much of. There was little, if any, reciprocal Royal interest in things Catholic. True enough, that kindly libertine Edward VII had refused to take the highly insulting Coronation oath against Popery, insisting on new wording—indeed as Prince of Wales he had visited Leo XIII long before such an action could have been justified diplomatically: the Pope was not then the head of an independent sovereign state. The visit to Italy and the Vatican in 1923 by George V and Queen Mary was gushingly celebrated in the magazine by Mother Mary Salome, who was in Rome at the time. (She had the double joy not only of writing up the Royal visit to the kingdom of Italy and to the Vatican, but also of reporting three Beatifications, one of which was of Thérèse of Lisieux.) "At last the King and Queen found themselves alone with the Holy Father. The audience lasted twenty-five minutes. Who shall say of what they spoke?" This is an interesting question; Pius XI was no conversationalist, and George V loathed being abroad: "Abroad is bloody. I know because I've been." Mother Mary Salome resumed her account by describing how "we vented our loyalty by decorating the main balcony with the Royal initials . . . This by no means exhausted our loyalty, so we sent a basket of very choice white roses, carnations and gardenias, with a parchment scroll." Years later when George VI died on February 6th 1952, it was noted that "Greatly envied by the rest of the school, the Sixth Form went to the lying-in-state . . . On February 15th lessons were stopped so that we could all listen in to the broadcast of the King's funeral." In 1977, at the time of the Silver Jubilee of our present Queen, there

was a special service in chapel, with many celebrations afterwards."
A few privileged people watched the Trooping of the Colour from
the forecourt of Buckingham Palace, and others the Garter Procession from the Lower Ward of Windsor Castle." The 15-year-old
Camilla Ballinger wrote that

> Even though our country is bankrupt and full of immorality and
> hideous blocks of flats, everything is forgotten when one sees
> the splendour and nobility of any of the celebrations of the Mon-
> archy. People say that it is far too expensive for England to sup-
> port, but I disagree. Maybe the cost has doubled, but so have all
> the other prices—British Rail tea for instance—and the Monarchy
> is worth more than British Rail tea. And I do feel most strongly
> that our Monarchy makes Britain.

The school magazine, like almost every such publication was,
and is, meticulous in reporting external and internal examination
results, along with public and internal awards and prizes. These
matter as a record of the school's growing involvement in the public
examinations field, and clearly they have always mattered to the
girls, parents and staff involved. Here it is appropriate to notice
landmarks, keeping in mind that until the 1940s, parents were not
looking for academic distinction. In 1948, as we have noted, Antonia
Pakenham and Elizabeth Rogers were awarded State Scholarships,
the first in the school's history. The list of achievements of that year
in the Oxford Higher Certificate, the Oxford School Certificate, the
Associated Board of the Royal Schools of Music is also impressive.
Girls took Pitman's Commercial Examinations, courses in First Aid
and Home Nursing, and the printed results of the monthly com-
petitions organised by the National Society of French Teachers
noted how many prizes were awarded.

It was during Mother Bridget's headship that external examinations came to be taken really seriously, and the establishment of a
proper Sixth Form has been noticed already. This is a development
that, if tabulated, would shew a rising curve, until one reaches the

extraordinary achievements listed in the magazine of 1992: forty in the top grades at A Level, thirty-five at A/S Level, forty-three at GCSE.

It is now an ordinary assumption that girls will proceed into one form or another of higher education, often with a list of dazzling accomplishments to their names. Whereas once, the battle was to persuade pupils to enter a proper Sixth Form, now in more recent years, the battle has been to persuade them to stay on at Ascot for Sixth Form study, rather than to leave to move to what may have been seen as the freer and more exciting world of the large boys' Independent Schools, or of the Sixth Form Colleges (which have the added attraction of being non-fee-paying). The building of the Mary Ward Court, the list of over twenty subjects on offer at A Level, and a very wide range of visits, with much greater freedom and independence are winning the battle at present. In 1991, the A Level Pass Rate was 98%, of which 83% were grades A to C. In 1992 the A Level Pass Rate was 99%, of which 87% were grades A to C; in 1993 there has been a Pass Rate of 100%, in the first three grades. St Mary's has become a school of nationally outstanding achievement.

But under Mother Bridget, as now, the chief purpose of the school was still seen to be to transmit a Catholic cultural heritage, religious and secular. It sufficed then, that this transmission was by a process of osmosis, invisible but assured, and the school, like the Catholic world in general, was a closed society. It is already difficult to remember many of its features, the multiplicity of devotions, the feast days and fast days, the largely unchallenged position of the clergy in a paternalistic Church. (Ascot was maternalistic, but it revolved around priests.) All these elements are amply recorded and reflected in the magazine, and the winds and gales of change in the 1960s seem to have had little impact. There were difficulties about hairstyles and stiletto heels. Mods and Rockers were on the horizon, but made their disturbances well away from the grounds, and the liturgical changes in the Mass that began to dribble through from 1968 onwards do not seem to have caused much commotion. The re-ordering of the Sanctuary in the school Chapel did occasion

Sister Bridget, 1993.

Cows in the Music School.

Mother Cecilia Marshall in 1955.

Members of the Community at Ascot,
year unknown (all identified, as Sisters
in modern usage, by Sister Bridget).
Back row (left to right): Sr Benedict, Sr
Peter, Sr John, Sr Margaret Mary, Sr
Ancilla, Sr Bernadette, Sr Barbara Barry,
Sr Hilary.
Middle row; Sr Emmanuel, Sr Mercedes,
Sr Alphonsa, Sr Perpetua, Sr Bonaven-
tura, Sr Campion, Sr Etheldreda, Sr Bar-
bara Bertini, Sr Isabelle.
Front row; Sr Regina, Sr John Baptist, Sr
Theresa, Sr Colette, Sr Cecily.

Top dormitory before the fire of August 15th 1986.

Mother Perpetua (seated left) and Mother Magdalen (right), with Mother
Isabelle, in charge of Errollston, 1936 - 46; 1946 - 53; 1953 - 70.

Opposite page:
Left: Sister Gregory Kirkus,
with a Bosnian child refugee
at the Bar Convent in York, 1993.
Right: Sister Gillian Orchard, 1993.
Below: The original swimming pool
built by Mother Cecilia.

Mlle Arlette Kalflèche, 1993.

Mrs Rhian Amery, 1994.

Mrs Clare Davies, 1993.

Group Captain
Philip Callan,
1993.

Sister Mark Orchard as a novice, 1963.

Sister Mark "topping out" Harewell House, Winter 1991.

Sister Mark (now Sister Frances), 1994.

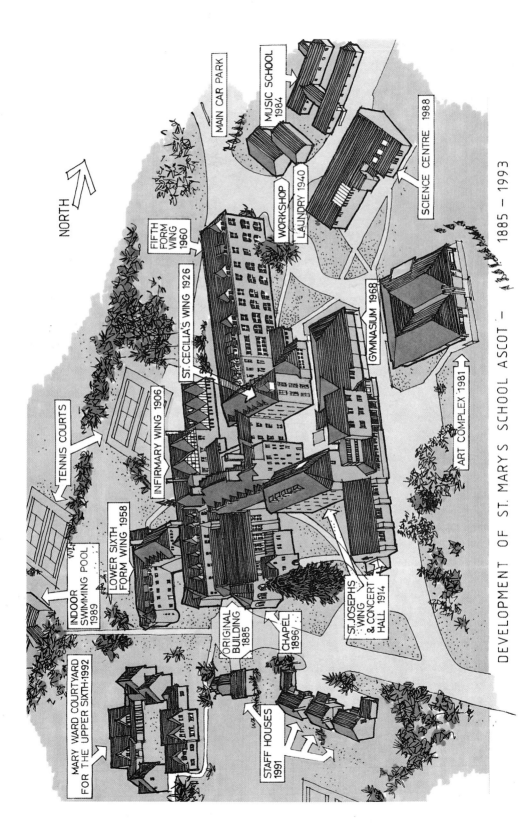

NORTH

MARY WARD COURTYARD
FOR THE UPPER SIXTH 1992

TENNIS COURTS

INDOOR
SWIMMING POOL
1989

LOWER SIXTH
FORM WING 1958

INFIRMARY WING 1906

ST. CECILIA'S WING 1926

FIFTH
FORM
WING
1960

MAIN CAR PARK

MUSIC SCHOOL
1984

WORKSHOP

LAUNDRY 1940

SCIENCE CENTRE 1988

GYMNASIUM 1968

ART COMPLEX 1981

ST.JOSEPHS
WING
& CONCERT
HALL 1914

CHAPEL
1896

ORIGINAL
BUILDING
1885

STAFF HOUSES
1991

DEVELOPMENT OF ST. MARYS SCHOOL ASCOT — 1885 – 1993

some disquiet, which can be encountered still, but most opinion seemed to think that the simplification and the removal of much decoration was an improvement: the greatest regret for some was replacing very comfortable benches by more seating for the growing school.

In 1964, a girl in the magazine commented that "We were let out into the big bad world with the usual warning: 'No brown paper parcels on the school train'." This was a reminder that ladies did not carry personal luggage, except elegantly. Indisputably 1968 is a dramatically key year in Catholic history; it was the year of *Humanae Vitae*. The magazine did mention that there was mischief abroad in the world and that "hardly any parents realise fully the dangers of the more-than-permissive society into which their children step so blithely and with such high ideals." So the permissive society got mentioned, but *Humanae Vitae* did not. Nor did it become a major element for discussion in Religious Education, so far as I can find out; such matters were in the hands of the Sisters, and there were no written schemes of work.

A quite different, but very prominent theme in the school magazine is how the Sisters unfailingly put the life and example of Mary Ward before the girls, in particular the efforts to promote her Beatification and Canonisation. The desire of the IBVM to proceed seems to have gathered momentum from 1924, when Mgr Redmond, the Vice-Rector in the English College in Rome, was named Postulator, that is the official chief pleader of the Cause. Cardinals came and went as Protectors, including the future Pius XII; it was important to have great names for this position. In 1932, there is the puzzling remark that "if the title of 'Venerable' had not been abolished, it would have been granted to her". The puzzle lies in the fact that it was granted to John Henry Newman in 1991. In 1933, Pius XI expressed the earnest wish that her Beatification should take place during his Pontificate. It did not, and so the work went on. The 300th anniversary of Mary Ward's death in 1945 was marked by a Pontifical High Mass in the school chapel, celebrated by that perennial visitor Archbishop Godfrey and six priests. In 1953 the Vocations

Exhibition at Olympia had a stand designed "to bring Mary Ward to the notice of thousands of people who had never heard of her". All through these years, appeals were made from pulpits, asking for all possible documentation to be sent in. Slowly a sense creeps in that nothing was going anywhere very much.

In the 1960s Mother Perpetua, the Provincial, became increasingly reluctant to send money to Rome for what seemed an interminable procedure. The centre of the matter was the requirement of "miracles of the first class, where the case must be hopeless as far as natural means of curing the disease are concerned, and a doctor must certify that it is so". A Jesuit priest, Father Grisar, worked most intensively over many years on this Cause. In the school itself, as well as many contributions to the magazine about Mary Ward, too numerous to be listed, a special prize essay was commissioned in 1959, on "The Personality and Spirituality of Mary Ward as seen from her Maxims", and was won by C. Elliott aged 13. (This was Claudia, grand-daughter of Sir Claude Elliott, Head Master and then Provost of Eton.) It may be that the English are not very good at miracles. They seem to abound in Mediterranean countries but not here. Newman's Cause languishes in the same way, whereas there is considerable momentum to canonize Pius IX, of all people. I remember an incident at Ampleforth in 1989, at a conference during which the Franciscan Father Guardian at Medjugorje spoke about the appearances of Our Lady there. This provoked a furious outburst from an enraged Englishman: "This is all about visions and miracles. We're English and we don't need them."

The 400th anniversary of Mary Ward's birth and the centenary of the school's foundation fell in 1985. There was a Mass of thanksgiving at Westminster Cathedral celebrated by Cardinal Hume, a Prize Day attended by Archbishop Worlock, and an essay in the magazine by Sister Bridget on "Ascot 1885 to 1985", followed by an article by Sister Emmanuel on Mary Ward herself. People with whom I have spoken who have been in the school at different times are unanimous in thinking that Mary Ward has been dealt with soberly and sanely—except for one young newcomer to the school who wrote in 1972: "Yesterday we celebrated the birthday of someone called St Ward who invented this place. I wish she hadn't."

I wrote to Sister Immolata Wetter, who until recently was the General Superior of the IBVM in Rome, to ask her where the Cause of Mary Ward had got to. She replied:

It has now reached the following stage: the preparatory work for the "Positio", to be presented to the Congregation for the Causes of Saints has now been completed; it runs into thousands of pages, including all the documents. The typing on computer is nearing its end. There still remains the "Informatio", which is a kind of introduction, mainly written by the official "Relator" of the Cause. Once the whole work is finished and printed, it will be handed over to the above-mentioned Congregation for the final judgement. The work as a whole has already been approved by the Relator of the Roman Congregation of the IBVM.

So there it is. I detect no great enthusiasm about all this amongst many members of the IBVM here. On the one hand there is a strong conviction that they know already how great was Mary Ward and simply want to get on with her work, but on the other hand just a whiff, perhaps even more than a whiff, of a feeling that it is irrelevant what some men in Rome finally decide about her.

7

The Headships of Sister Emmanuel and Sister Mark, 1976 to 1993

From 1961 onwards, lay teachers may have been appointed in increasing numbers to full-time positions but, as has been made plain, they were still seen as ancillary, as visitors with clearly defined and circumscribed duties. The school, in the details of its discipline, the elaborateness of its clothing requirements and regulations, and the sense of keeping the world at arm's length was, so it seems in retrospect, saturated in nuns. It was their view—there were no dissentient voices—that was enunciated, on the place of women in society, on the married state, on religious, moral and ethical matters. There was some very good, some exceptional teaching, and girls were going in increasing numbers into higher education, but generally the girls were not stretched. As one of them put it: "We were not encouraged to be ambitious".

One of the aims of this book has always been to see the school in all kinds of contexts. 1976 was mid-point in the decade in which Britain slid into ever-deepening political and economic troubles. There were the miners' strikes, there was the "three-day week", there were power cuts; there was also the national debate about Britain's membership of the European Community—a membership negotiated by the Heath Government, and put to the only referendum so far in our political history by the Wilson Government. The growing political and economic troubles led many people to believe that the country was in terminal decline, and Denis Healey, as Chancellor of the Exchequer, was compelled to ask the IMF for an immense loan, for which he was obliged to raise the National Interest Rate to 15%. In 1978/1979 we experienced the "Winter of

Discontent", when the streets were unswept, the rubbish uncollected, and the dead unburied on Merseyside. Many people thought that the management of the country was sliding out of control and felt bruised in one way or another by these last ten years. The General Election of 1979 brought in a Conservative Government with Mrs Thatcher as Prime Minister.

Not only was there political and economic disturbance, but also great unrest in the educational world. The "great white hope" of the 1960s—the Schools Council—had been seen by many people, certainly by Mrs Thatcher, as a misplaced institution, which was heading for disbandment. The Comprehensive School, propounded as the only socially acceptable way of organising children's secondary schooling, came increasingly to be criticised. I have referred already to the speech at Oxford, in which the Prime Minister, James Callaghan, drew national attention to these growing misgivings, and his Secretary of State, Shirley Williams, organised a nation-wide series of discussions and debates as to how policy should be developed. It is true that the Local Education Authorities and their schools were the most affected by these developments, but independent schools could not but be aware of them, and had to reconsider their own circumstances.

In the private sector the most obvious of all effects was of inflation on school fees. In one school, just as an example, fees in 1970 were £609 a year; in 1975, they jumped three times, from £1,278 to £1,479 to £1,575. In April 1980 they were £2,800, a year later £3,600. By September of 1990, they were £9,400 (and at the time of writing this, £12,000). Another major development in schools in the public sector was the emergence of a defined path to promotion, through the establishment of departments or faculties and the creation of management structures; it became highly unlikely that anyone would be promoted to headship who had not gone through these stages. For the teaching body as a whole, in-service training, nationally, regionally and school-based, became part of almost every teacher's life, accompanied by a very large number of publications on every aspect of schooling. Such questions as "What do you mean by a good school?" and "Do schools make any difference?" were explored with more precision than before. Change, and change again became the way of life, and had its impact on initial teacher training—for example, the acceptance of the idea of the "all-graduate profession". Most independent schools of note took part in many of these developments. The debates and publications of the Headmasters' Conference and of the Girls' Schools Association illustrate this, and most of the independent denominational schools were as active as the rest.

It was in these years that "the Ascot of the Nuns" ended with the departure of Mother Bridget. I think it is fair to say that the school seems barely to have noticed what was going on. Sister Catherine was responsible for keeping the books for wages and salaries, and Sister John Baptist meticulously recorded the incidental expenses of every pupil. The Sisters were not paid, and each lay individual on the staff had a privately negotiated contract. This, on many occasions, ran along the following lines: "As you will remember when we talked, you agreed to . . . and Wednesday is your shopping day, and children have to be taken to and from school, and Thursday is your golf day". Salaries did not automatically go up every year, and there was no incremental scale related to the national system. It appears that no financial records survive from before the time of computers. I am reminded here of the delightfully revealing comment by one Sister, when crisis eventually descended: "Do remember, my dear, it's only money". In these circumstances Sister Emmanuel became headmistress. She writes

On Palm Sunday 1976 I was summoned by Reverend Mother Provincial (Mother Gregory) and "invited" to take responsibility for the school at Ascot, on Mother Bridget's retirement. I spent Holy Week in a state of shock and numbness. How did I begin to take over from somone who had been in office for twenty years, and whose style and way of dealing with things were all her own? She left a wonderfully tidy desk, drawers all-but empty, just a few letters pertaining to prospective pupils and past glories. If

I'd hoped for some sort of induction into the mysteries of head-ship, I was barking up the wrong tree.

So begins a memoir to me from Sister Gillian, who was at that time Sister Emmanuel, a delightful and honest account of her period as headmistress.

These were the years of transition, based on a recognition that changes of all kinds needed to be made. A Religious Institute, committed to school education, had not consciously studied the trends and changes that were taking place all around. Until then there had been no need to do so. The school still provided very much what most of its parents wanted, but young people were beginning to have new hopes and expectations. It was government policy to increase greatly the number of places in higher education; a range of new universities was being created, some of which, for a time, were seen as the height of fashion. 1968 was the year of student rebellion and of *Humanae Vitae*. The contraceptive pill brought a host of opportunities and problems and posed the most searching questions to those involved in Catholic moral instruction. For example, doctors were not obliged to inform parents if they had prescribed the pill, even for girls under sixteen. Therefore, in the light of all this, to ask a Sister—who had gone from school at Ascot into the Novitiate at Ascot and so to final Profession, taking a university degree and a teacher-training certificate on the way, returning to teach in the same school—simply to assume the headship, shewed up structural weakness in the Institute.

Sister Emmanuel/Gillian says that she was told to do things her way.

I realised that I needed, even if no-one else realised it, the support and advice of professional bodies on how to administer an expanding school efficiently and effectively. I renewed subscriptions to the relevant associations, attended meetings and conferences, and began to use such services as were offered, and encouraged the teaching staff, lay and religious, to do the same.

In a short time, I came to know and appreciate the positive encouragement that the teaching profession provides for its members. By contrast, at the same time, I experienced the apparent lack of interest from the one body which, as a Religious, I sought support, namely the IBVM Provincial Council.

She found that the Council did not, and did not seem to wish to, see itself as a governing body. She regularly sent in reports on the school but received no worthwhile response.

In humility, she also recognised that she was not an administrator, and that at a time when so much of the helpful new office gadgetry had not come in, and matters still depended on personal copying and filing.

More than anything else, with her headship there was a change of style. This reflected many of the changes in the Church and in Religious Orders and Congregations coming out of Vatican II, but it was also in keeping with her own personality and her own approach to other people. The days of certainty and a sense of, perhaps, superior separateness were passing rapidly from the clergy and the Orders. Many of them were going through deep crises; men and women left the religious life and there was a falling-off in vocations. For many it was a distressing time, for others there was a sense of new openings and beginnings. Sister Emmanuel was one of those who welcomed change, and saw it as liberation. The spirit of Cecilia Marshall had permeated everything long enough; the separation of the Sisters from the lay staff needed to be diminished, if not ended. She therefore began to call regular full teaching staff meetings, and to loosen up relationships; colloquia on particular themes were held. The headmistress was approachable and loved the company of the girls. She was only the headmistress; the rest of the IBVM structure remained untouched; for example, the Superior was still finally responsible for the school; the Provincial still lived on the site. Sister Agatha, as Superior, supported Sister Emmanuel in her educational work, though the school's finances, and its building programme were not the headmistress's responsibility. It was in these years that the IBVM, as a religious body, entered into much self-scrutiny about what its true purposes should be, and about whether it should be carrying out other work than teaching the daughters of the rich. Some of the more important members of the Institute were not especially sympathetic to Ascot. The idea that it should represent "the best" was questioned. One obvious result of all this was the decrease in the number of Sisters teaching in the school.

The matter of the "daughters of the rich" needs a little elaboration. It was in Mother Bridget's time that entry was broadened to bring in more girls from families not hitherto connected with the school. In her judgement, this introduced not only new blood but new talent, and lived up to the internationalism for which the Institute was supposed to stand. This policy, and the rapidly changing attitudes of young people, were going to make it increasingly difficult to continue with the elaborate rules and old attitudes. Furthermore, the liturgical reforms of Vatican II were being introduced into Church worship, and their general effect was to simplify and demystify. Sister Emmanuel saw that it would be wise to tone down the rigidities of required religious observance, and to seek for their essential spirit and meaning through simpler forms. In an article in the Jesuit journal, *The Way*, in an issue devoted entirely to the matter of celibacy in the Catholic Church, she has shewn how, in her own emotional and religious development she was moving away from some of the patterns of thought and practice into which she had been Professed in 1961. She recognised the trend of the times, and that the spiritual life of the staff and of the girls would have to be explored and developed and newly approached. She gave a great deal of thought to pastoral work in the school—which her Superiors, at a later time, have been wise enough to deploy throughout all the schools of the Province.

I remember a phrase desciding the pontificate of Pope Leo IX in the eleventh century: "It abounded in beginnings". So did Sister Emmanuel's headship. As her health began seriously to deteriorate, she was able to appoint a Deputy Head, the first in the school's history. Julia Makin was a laywoman, a Christian but not a Catholic, married with a family, and with special qualifications in Personnel Management. In a calm and imperturbable manner, she was able to help put into practice what the headmistress intended. With her, Sister Emmanuel began to explore what was being written and discussed in the educational world about desirable curriculum change, realising increasingly that the staffing of the school would have to be put onto a different basis if anything substantial were intended; the world of individual contracts and variable hours would have to be tackled.

It would seem that above everything else she thought that relationships in the Institute at Ascot, and between Sisters and lay staff, needed to be re-shaped; "informality" does not sum things up, but indicates how she wanted things to go. Because she felt deeply problems in the religious life, she put immense energy into the school. "I knew that I was not cut out for the task, but I could not have persuaded anyone. The job was too much; in the end my body took charge of the situation." She became critically ill, and had to give up her work.

"I was a write-off as far as the school was concerned, except as a focus for its compassion and prayer", Sister Gillian has written to me. It is marvellous to be able to record that she recovered and went on to other posts of responsibility within the Institute. I have benefited greatly from her help and advice and most of all from her friendship. She herself wanted to conclude her comments to me with some words from Mary Ward:

> If you feel in yourself a desire to perform a virtuous work very profitable to the greater honour of God but have no opportunity of fulfilling it, rejoice if others bring it to pass instead of you. For if God is served, what does it matter from whom He will receive the service?

These words, most moving in themselves, and telling so much of the goodness of Sister Gillian, form a perfect transitional passage to the next headship, that of her own sister, Sister Mark Orchard. If Sister Gillian's tenure were transitional, it was an absolutely necessary transition, a change of style and atmosphere.

The circumstances of Sister Mark's succession have a familiar ring about them: like her sister before her, and Sister Bridget before that, there was, apparently, "no-one else". She admits that she was neither surprised nor enthusiastic, not least when it was indicated to be a short-term appointment. "I detected a feeling that had circumstances been different I would not have been asked. Given my ignorance about schools in general and my knowledge about Ascot in particular, I suspected that the job was not going to be a sinecure." She knew that the lack of vocations over the previous twenty years was undermining the traditional structures of the school; there was tension within the Community at Ascot between those who wanted no change, and those who wanted to pull out and move directly into ministries associated with "the option for the poor". She wrote down a simple plan of action for herself: "to restructure the school to ensure that if and when the IBVM has neither the ability nor the inclination to run a boarding school for girls it will pass smoothly into the hands of the Catholic laity". She had a great ally in Sister Denis, the Superior, who soon made it clear that it was the headmistress who had authority in the school, and so broke with traditional practice.

> The ship almost sank in my first few months from the accumulation of poor financial management together with an admirable but naive spirit of "the right hand not knowing what the left hand was doing". I knew that there was no such thing as a school budget, but this did not prevent me from asking to see it. I was given a piece of paper on which was written the cost of lay salaries ten years previously and their cost in 1982. No other costs were available. Expenditure was an unknown fact. Outgoings were in excess of income, and this at a time when no salaries were paid to IBVM Sisters working in the school, no rent was paid, and the fee level bore no resemblance to services rendered.

Sister Mark's comments on the tension that was to grow up between the Institute and the new governing body, soon to be formed, were that there was a difference of perception between the two. The governors had a clear sense of their new responsibilities, and the IBVM no longer had a clearly defined vision. In a letter, in which she reflected over the ten years of her headship, she wrote about this problem as she saw it at the time: "What do the IBVM want? Do we want to regard the school as a sound business investment that produces a fixed income for the increasingly ageing IBVM or do we see the school as the vehicle for continuing the educational work that the IBVM is no longer able or willing to do?" Before her first term began, she wrote to parents to announce her first changes. Her introduction was humorous:

> Soon after Pope John XXIII was elected he was asked what he intended to do. He replied that he would watch and listen but for the time being do nothing. Who else better to imitate, I thought, on receiving a somewhat lesser mandate from our Provincial earlier this year? However, within months, you will recall, Pope John made known his intention to call the Second Vatican Council, and the Church has never been the same since. The purpose of this letter is not to summon you to an ecumenical Council, so you can relax, but to let you know of various changes that I feel impelled to introduce now.

So the new style came in, and she proceeded to ask for an outside assessment of the school by Norbert Winstanley, who was the Advisor on Secondary Education to the Catholic Education Council. When he was invited to "review and comment on aspects of education at St Mary's", he brought a team consisting of: Angela Lawrence, Religious Education Advisor to the Diocese of Arundel and Brighton; John Doyle, Secretary of the Schools' Commission of the Diocese of Portsmouth, and John Hampson, Director of Schools for the Diocese of Hexham and Newcastle. These titles hid, rather than declared, a wealth of educational experience over the whole range of schools and colleges. It was a team that had already carried out similar visits in other Catholic schools. Its method was not to inspect in the sense that H.M. Inspectors would work, that is by concentrating on a detailed examination of what went on in the classrooms, putting it against the expressed intentions of the school. In this case, a mixture of techniques was used, of seeing some class-work, of talking with groups of teachers, but of offering to every teacher, religious and lay, the opportunity for personal confidential discussion. On re-reading the Report, I have been struck again by the sensitive but immensely detailed nature of the enquiry; people certainly opened their hearts. Much of this, therefore, could not be written up, but only reported on verbally and to a lesser extent in writing to the new headmistress and the Superior of the House. In the written report, it was stated that "It would be naive to think that the team had been invited into the school to affirm that everything was perfect . . . The Report is offered as an honest and genuine appraisal . . . The Report, though critical in many aspects, is offered in the spirit of true friendship and Christian love." As I explained in the Introduction to this book, I joined in much of the work of the team, but not all, was present at the extended reporting afterwards, and became one of the first governors of a Board whose creation was seen in the Report as "imperative and urgent".

The immediate background to the visit was of financial problems resulting from an extensive building programme, carried out by a school that had no bursarial organisation and no firm grip on income and expenditure. The recommended Board was therefore to have "overall financial and material responsibility for the school: to determine fees; to prepare standardised contracts for all employees, including all teaching staff".

The school was said to suffer from a lack of clear, well-defined, published aims; oral practice and tradition would no longer be enough. Each department in the school should be required to produce detailed statements of purpose, and of the methods proposed to achieve them. An unfair and irrational distribution of duties existed that put far too much strain on some teachers, especially in the Community. The general message of the Report was that of rationalisation, balance, standardisation, and openness in management. A great deal of attention was given to Pastoral Care, with many recommendations made.

The Report provided Sister Mark with a base line for her work, and in the following years she implemented everything in it and much more. In doing this, she became the first fully professional headmistress of the school, able to make St Mary's the outstanding independent Catholic girls' school in the country.

The first great change came when the Community left the main building and moved to Errollston. The significance of this was vastly more than is contained in such a simple sentence. The Sisters, even when the Community was large, had lived in the same building as the girls, and though there were the "no-go areas" that are part of any convent, the intermingling of lives was an everyday matter, and the girls saw a living Community in practice. It has been noticed often that Provincial and Superior and Headmistress were all in the same house. Errollston is some distance away, and when the Provincial and Superior went to live there, it left, at last, the Headmistress as the real presence in the school. The Superior's position itself as Principal has meant less and less, until it has became titular. When Sister Pia succeeded Sister Francis as Provincial in 1991, and decided to move the Provincialate to Hampstead, the break became more obvious.

The building of new houses next to the school, justified as part of the policy of preparing for lay management, took place after many arguments with the local planning authority, and Sister Mark moved into one of them. She was made answerable to the Provincial in London rather than to the Superior in Errollston. This was the end of an era. The headmistress, ably served by an outstanding secretary, Mrs Clare Davies, with an increasing ancillary staff, with a well-furnished study and herself skilled in new technologies, with a house across the way for entertaining, became a figure comparable to the heads of other important girls' schools. Her membership of the Girls' Schools Association and of other professional bodies brought her onto the national stage.

As well as a Board of Governors the Winstanley Report recommended the appointment of a full-time bursar, to take over the previous rather sketchy supervision of the buildings, the catering and the estate. Group Captain Philip Callan speedily became the most important figure in the school's life next to the headmistress.

The number of Sisters teaching in the school has diminished. Sister Michaela, with her unsurpassed gift of loving and caring for the younger pupils, has become the only full-time teaching Sister on the staff. All departmental heads are lay, including that for Religious Education. For all the gains in these changes, many present and past pupils regret the diminishing presence of the Sisters; only in their first two years do the girls now feel enfolded, "mothered", so that home-sickness—as I was told by the girls themselves—is not a major problem. This is Sister Michaela's achievement. It is perhaps all that is left of the old pattern.

Many believe that a price has been paid for the increasing separation of the Community from the school. Sarah Hogg's point, reinforced by others, was that she came to realise that she was, for a short time, a member of a "an undying community" (as the medieval lawyers regarded religious houses). Olga Polizzi has also said to me that such a community includes the living, the dying and the dead. She felt that in her day they were taught not to be afraid of death. In the Errollston pamphlet for October 1992, there is a reference to "Sister Baptist, who has looked after the health of the Community with wonderful devotion, and saw Sisters Perpetua, Mercedes and De Sales off to their heavenly home."

O Death, where is thy sting, O Grave, thy victory?

Girls observing the Community would have seen that all was not always sweetness and light; in the name of the greater good, compromises had to be made, difficulties in personality accommodated. But this was part of their education. The Community has had a sense of purpose from Mary Ward's time onwards, and from this came vocations, a call to the service of God through the education of girls. One reason for the falling-off in vocations is thought, in part, to come from a sense of loss of purpose in the Institute. It is not the whole story; there have been dramatic changes in the circumstances in girls' and women's lives. No longer is it a matter of being either a good Catholic wife and mother, or a nun, but rather of identifying which way to serve God in the multiplicity of ways now open, in and through higher and further education and beyond. In talking to present-day Sixth Formers in the school, this point was made to me persuasively, movingly and in many instances, humbly.

The withdrawal of the Franciscans from the parish in 1980, which they had served since its foundation, led the school to ask the incoming secular parish priest to act as chaplain. When, in 1991, the parish priest, Fr Brian Murphy O'Connor, moved elsewhere, Fr Ian Ker was appointed part-time chaplain to the school, residing in Frith Cottage on the estate. The chief purpose was to have a celebrant and a confessor; religious education, and its connection with personal and social development—now a required theme in the National Curriculum—has been made the responsibility of teachers within the school. The departure of Fr Ian, and the appointment of his successor, Fr Dermot Power, will open up opportunities for a considerable amount of further thought on how to develop the chaplaincy. Chaplains are not likely to be professionally-trained teachers, and they may not wish to be timetabled to teach; they will certainly become more actively involved in the school.

The range of buildings and facilities now provided, powerfully enhanced by the results of two School Appeals, have transformed the appearance and comfort of the place. A new, very fully equipped Science Block is part of a policy of enticing girls into the sciences. A new Art Block, with an increased number of teachers, has already opened up an ever-widening range of activities, including an astonishingly rapid development in photography. A magnificent covered and heated swimming pool has replaced the one built by Mother Cecilia that was thought to be so advanced in its day. It was opened by Olga Polizzi/Forte, who allowed herself to be

thrown in as some sort of symbolic gesture. The story so far con-
cludes with the building of the Mary Ward Courtyard, so splendid
that it could be run as a small hotel. The school is now in a good
position to attract outside conferences in the holidays. For example,
the General Congregation of the Roman Generalate of the IBVM
was held there in the July and August of 1993, with multilingual
interpreting facilities.

Sixth Formers relish living in the Mary Ward Courtyard. They
think they have about enough freedom, though they have some
reservations about the controlled arrangements for meeting boys
from other schools or young men from outside. They can entertain
them, and public formal dances are arranged with Eton, Wellington, Worth and other schools, no doubt with all the self-conscious
awkwardnesses and premature sophistication that such occasions
tend to generate.

The girls with whom I talked felt that the school had "got it right"
about Mary Ward and Cecilia Marshall. I was surprised to be told
that they thought they needed more direct instruction and information than they had received, about the formal teaching of the
Church through its *magisterium*. They appreciated just how much
pastoral care they had had on the way through the school, and did
not seem to resent that they were being most carefully watched—
not least for signs and symptoms of anorexia nervosa and bulimia.
Talking with girls in the middle and lower school, I met once again
the sentiment that has run through this book, that they have been
and are happy, though some of them said that weekends can drag a
bit. They accepted as completely normal that all pupils are required
to take Religious Education as a subject for the GCSE examination.
Requirements about Mass attendance have changed dramatically
since the old days. Mass is obligatory only on Sundays, and as the
chapel cannot hold everyone, senior girls are expected to go to the
parish church. (Why not two Masses?) Pretty well all else is voluntary.

The only significant remaining school ritual that I could find concerned "Peanuts": you must not, ever, pull your socks up or fasten

the top button of your shirt. To do so is to be cast into outer darkness. In truth, the last real survival of the old days when the lay Sisters did everything for them, is the work of Sister Gabriel in the laundry. Every pupil has a number which is attached to every item of clothing. Sister Gabriel knows every number, and clothes are washed or cleaned, repaired, ironed and returned in perfect condition; the laundry is one of the main places where the girls meet and talk freely with the Sisters.

A common room filled with lay people, a staff refectory in which all teachers eat—from a remarkable choice of menu every day— staff meetings, in-service training days, attendance at courses and conferences, staff appraisal, the development of new subjects, a full curriculum and a dazzling record of academic achievement put the school at a far remove from that to which Mlle Kalflèche came in 1961 to teach French or Mrs Wilson in 1971 to teach Mathematics.

I have stressed the words "happy" and "happiness" often in this narrative, for good reason. Schools, even the best, always have a record of some people who were miserably unhappy there, to the extent that their whole recollection is unbalanced and poisoned, lacking objectivity in judgement. It has been amazing to meet so many former pupils, from many decades, who have insisted on their happiness at Ascot. Perhaps this feeling is most concentrated on the days when the Sisters ran every aspect of the school; it is their dedication and love that seems to have suffused their pupils' lives, and it may be that the more transient nature of a lay staff, not necessarily Catholic, with all its potential for professionalism and academic qualifications, may not be able to provide the sense of permanence and security that the old Community gave. One of our contributors wrote of her own time at Ascot: "I was so happy that I sent my daughter to the school. But that is a different story." And, indeed, it has been important to investigate the views and feelings of those girls who have gone more recently through the school, the St Mary's Ascot Part Two, so to speak, the school ever more predominantly lay, with the elderly IBVM Sisters across the way at Errollston, no longer a continuing influence over the girls; everything, in other words, substantially dependent on the headmistress.

If the last ten years represent, as they most certainly do, the opening of a new phase in the school's history, this has not arrived effortlessly, without argument or tension. The governing Board has had to sort out its relationship with the Institute, and the Institute with the governing Board. The Institute owns the school, and leases it to the Board. The Board wishes to buy out the lease, so that it can manage affairs with complete responsibility; but if this were to happen, the Institute would lose all real connection with the school. Over the last ten years, the headmistress has had to become professionally sensitive to and aware of tumultuous educational and social changes in that period. This has demanded an enormous amount of her time, with unavoidable tensions and pressures on her life as a Religious, of which she has been well aware. Her 1993/1994 sabbatical—though probably too long—was deserved and needed. The very success of the school could be likened, so to speak, to the results of throwing a large brick into the IBVM pond, where the splashes and ripples have been considerable.

To move from a teaching staff entirely of Religious to one mostly lay has brought the predictable problems of staff recruitment and appointment in a district of great wealth and expensive housing; it has put the school into the position of depending on the likelihood that professional families living in the district have professional graduate wives and mothers willing to teach full-time or part-time in the school. The simple arrangements of olden days, with no budget, no accounts, maintenance by old faithful retainers and a vast amount of work carried out by the unpaid lay Sisters has given way to a completely professional administration and estate management run by an extended bursarial office. Detailed accounts of income and expenditure have to be presented to the governing Board, and there are people on it who understand them. The school is a business that has to look to its profitability. The chairmanship of the Board is a centrally important element in the life of the school, and Julian Bell (1984 to 1989) and John Albert (1989 onwards) have been masters of their craft. All these factors can be seen in a study of the minutes of Governors' meetings, to which I now want to turn. They may be confidential but that does not make them the most gripping reading that an outsider might want to have. However, they get at much of the truth—not the whole truth—of the last decade.

The transition from the old days was begun by a management committee that met at various times from January to November 1984. It was then that the IBVM had to work out how to create and hand over to a governing Board, and to support the new head-mistress as she began the rationalisation of teaching contracts and the best use of time in the school. Right at the beginning, in January, Sister Mark was concerned to reduce over-teaching in certain sub-jects, to produce a less hurried learning environment, to give more time to extra-curricular activities and to make better use of staffing.

The first meeting of the new governing Board was held on 12th November 1984 at Ascot. For the record, the Board consisted of: Sis-ter Francis (Provincial), Sister Denis (Superior at Ascot), Sister James, Sister Mark, Julian Bell as Chairman, Neil Merritt, John Buckenham, Father Butterworth sj, Sarah Hogg and Roy Wake. Clare Davies was asked and agreed to serve as clerk until a bursar were appointed, and Sister Denis, as local Superior, was to act as bursar until the post was properly filled. It was seen immediately that the following year, the 400th anniversary of the birthday of Mary Ward, should be the occasion for a major Appeal to extend the facilities of the school. This first meeting, and quite a number to follow, was preoccupied with establishing what would be the appro-priate rental that the governors should pay to the IBVM. For a time there was considerable tension between the expectations of the IBVM and the concerns of the governors, faced, as they were, with a host of problems, such as the state of buildings and estate, the hap-hazardry of staff contracts, and the matter—which would be a hardy annual—of staff salaries in relation to the national system. In May 1985 a finance and general purposes committee was created, to consist of governors who understood finance and management, and in the July of that year Group Captain Philip Callan was appointed as bursar, after a distinguished career in the Royal Air Force. The school was full, the 1986 entry list had been closed already, and indeed the list was over-booked.

It was also recognised at that meeting of the new governing Board that it was necessary to establish a proper bursary fund to ensure that intelligent and able students could be subsidised to enter the school, and to help in cases of disaster—business failures, unexpected deaths and so on. For the first, but not for the last time, the nature of the IBVM presence in the school that might be expected in the future was raised. Sister Francis stated that it was possible that three or four Sisters would still be at Ascot in five years' time, but it was also possible that there would be none; there was a lot of movement in the Community and the younger members were anxious to work in poorer, deprived areas. So it was clear from the beginning that the IBVM presence would diminish. The school was getting larger, and almost all positions of responsibility would begin to pass into lay hands.

The meeting in March 1986 thanked Julia Makin for all she had done as deputy head, and approved the appointment of Mrs Rhian Amery, already a member of the English staff, to be the new deputy head. The selection process once again highlighted the dearth of suitable Catholic applicants for teaching posts. This meeting also decided that the principal aim of the Centenary Appeal should be a new Science Block. Bernard Ashford, a distinguished professional appeals director, was appointed to the task. He said that £500,000 would be needed. Mrs Olga Polizzi agreed to be Chairman of the Appeal, and in fact she joined the governing Board. The next meeting, on 8th December, dealt in a surprisingly cool way with the great fire of August 15th 1986. This time Our Lady looked favourably on the school, but in a somewhat roundabout way, since the fire destroyed two dormitories and the pupils' refectory. The refectory was rebuilt and tenders sought for the reinstatement of the dormitories to the best modern standards. It was also planned to seize the opportunity to provide ten extra bedroom spaces. In other words, as a result of the fire and out of the insurance, the school emerged with better buildings—but, in the meantime, lived in quite extraordinary improvised accommodation. As in the War, the school rose to the occasion magnificently; under pressure, everyone lived cheerfully in difficult circumstances.

At this same meeting in December 1986, two of the most persistent concerns came up yet again: the matter of the rental, still rattling on, and the whole question of IBVM presence in the school. On the one hand, the Provincial's right and freedom to move Sisters as she thought fit was indisputably acknowledged, but on the other the problem of how much proper notice should be given to those who had to run the school, had to be established. Sister Francis, as Provincial, reiterated that there were no suitable Sisters available for school work, and that there was definitely no prospect that the IBVM could replace Sister Mark as headmistress.

By March 1987, it was clear that the Appeal would be over-subscribed, so that not only could a new Science Block be built, but also a further project could be considered. More than any other, there was enthusiasm for a completely modernised and covered swimming pool. Both projects were proceeded with. The new Science building was opened by Miss Sheila Browne, Principal of Newnham College Cambridge, and former Head of H.M. Inspectorate, in the October of 1988.

Succeeding meetings noted the completion of rebuilding after the fire, the insignificant damage to the school by the "great gale" of October 1987, and final agreement on the terms of the lease reached in February 1988. In that same year there was a record number of places gained at Oxford and Cambridge: out of 10 candidates 6 were successful with a further 2 who had recently left. From December 1988 Sister M. Pia joined the Board to represent Sister Francis. Future registrations showed a very high demand for places and the 1990 list was closed early. In 1989 there was an acute shortage of Sixth Form bedrooms in relation to the number of good quality direct-entry Sixth Form applicants; this situation had been (happily) aggravated by the decision by most Fifth Formers to remain at the school. In the February of 1989, Sister Mark put forward her plans for a Friends of St Mary's/Parents Support Group, to organise regional meetings all over the country, based in the homes of, or other venues offered by individual parents. This idea proved very successful, making it possible for parents to raise their concerns informally and in much smaller groups. It was also becoming clear by this time that, in planning for the future increasing lay control of the school, it was essential to be able to offer full and proper staff accommodation on the estate, not least because the Ascot area was one of such high-priced housing. In time, this led to the building of four houses and to other conversions and modernisations. The meeting in December 1989 was the last to be chaired by Julian Bell, and John Albert was elected as his successor.

By December 1990, Joan Jefferson, Headmistress of St Swithun's School Winchester, had joined the Board; the overall pass rate at A Level was 99+% and 55% achieved results in the A/B categories; six regional meetings of the St Mary's Ascot Support Group had been held; and a member of staff had been appointed "European Coordinator". There were worries expressed that a tendency in girls' schools to leave at sixteen was becoming noticeable at Ascot, and it was increasingly clear to the governors that something dramatic would have to be done to make staying on into the Sixth Form truly attractive. Out of this came the plan for a new Sixth Form Block, that was likely to be named after Mary Ward. The same meeting recorded the surprising lack of complaint from parents concerning the 21. 6% increase in school fees. This massive increase at long last made it possible for the school to finance a properly attractive salaries system for its teaching and administrative staff, and finally closed all those long years when fees could be modest and salaries haphazard because of the underpinning of the unpaid services of the IBVM Sisters. Those Sisters who now teach in the school are paid proper salaries.

The Appeal to build the Mary Ward Court was launched in January 1992, with Lady Cecil Cameron as Chairman, and Geoffrey van Cutsem, a governor, as Deputy Chairman. By March 1992, the number of acceptances for new places in the following September had exceeded expectations thus creating an accommodation problem: fifteen boarders over capacity and twenty-five over the budgeted figure. Rhian Amery was due to retire in August, and Monica Hehir was appointed to succeed her as deputy head. The Mary Ward Court was opened officially by the Rt. Hon. Christopher Patten on June 27th 1992. Sister Mark announced that she had been given permission by the Provincial Council to have a sabbatical from April 1st 1993 to 31st March 1994. The Council had also agreed that she should return to continue her headship up to September 1997. Rhian Amery agreed to come back as acting head during her time away. It was at this meeting that I was asked to write the history of the school. At the December meeting of 1992, it was reported that the percentage pass-rate of 99.1% at A Level was the highest ever recorded at St Mary's. At the last governors' meeting up to this point in writing, Sister Mark told us that there were many more candidates for entry at 11+ than there were places available, so a lengthy reserve list was created. There is to be an entry at 13+ in 1995, and entry at 10+ is to cease after 1994. The overall number for September 1993 is 343 on the roll.

This has been a highly selective extracting from nine years of meetings, simply to try to give a flavour of the challenges faced, and the business conducted. Essentially, it is a record of extraordinarily successful expansion, in numbers and in academic achievement. During these years, Sister Mark has rationalised and reorganised staffing, introducing staffing appraisal schemes and creating a senior management team. She has committed the school to the essentials of the National Curriculum, and indeed, to put it crudely, not missed a trick in any significant educational or management development. The extraordinary increase in buildings and amount of modernisation has been noted. It could be said that perhaps only two major issues still have to be decided upon, that of buying the lease from the IBVM, with all its implications for the Institute and for the school, and the building of a new Music School to meet the requirements of the outstanding developments in this field. Many would be delighted to see this last idea expanded into a project for a

Performing Arts Centre which would require a larger sum of money than any so far spent and, unavoidably, another Appeal. In the meantime, the existing Music School is being substantially rebuilt, to double its size, at a cost of £310,000; it should be ready for use towards the end of 1994.

8

The School Now and in the Future

It was long a received view amongst historians that there is a chronological point beyond which one cannot operate in accordance with generally accepted procedures. History ends and current affairs, or whatever one chooses to call them, begin. In this light, writing about Ascot up to the present year cannot be considered proper history. Any account of recent years in the school must be impressionistic, lacking in the perspective that only the passage of time can give, and more than usually open to dissent. I can say only that I have tried to listen to representative views, and to reflect on them in the light of knowledge built up about the earlier years. This is why there is perhaps a repetitive emphasis on "the Ascot of the Nuns", and on the opinion that the school is in a second phase of its history, with the third phase not far away, when it passes entirely into lay management. This has been my opinion, but I have encountered another, in which the present years are seen as very much an interim phase, with a rider that the sooner this ends, the better, so that the school can settle down properly to its future. Here, immediately, is an argument.

It would have been silly and unacceptable to have written this account from 1885 to 1965, but it is a long haul from 1885 to 1993, from a school of a handful of girls situated in thinly populated heathland, to a school of approaching 350 standing in a highly expensive residential area. No doubt the school could be bigger still, but no-one wants a larger school. It must be amply clear by now that the religious Institute that founded it, embraced and encompassed it until the 1960s. As Cathune Cape/Johnstone described it:

We lived surrounded by nuns. They taught us all the subjects except French and Gym and were present at all our activities: getting up, going to bed, and bed-making. They supervised our meals, the mid-morning break, walks outside the grounds and all our weekend and evening activities. We did not feel oppressed by this. On the contrary, we felt very sheltered, loved and cared for.

Catherine Devas/Nolan made the same point.

Ascot was like one huge family. Every single nun, even those we rarely saw, knew the name of each pupil. When Heather Fraser died in 1937 (she was 16), the entire Community mourned as though they had lost a member of their family. I announced my engagement in the August of 1948 (I left Ascot in 1940), and five of the nuns wrote to felicitate me, and sent me a tablecloth which they had embroidered themselves. Thirty-three years later, those same nuns, now living in convents elsewhere, wrote to comfort me on the death of our youngest son.

This is remembrance of times past. It is difficult to believe that no pupil was unhappy, but all who have written and spoken to me, have insisted on memories of happy and untroubled times. I was let into one confidential account of how one bewildered girl was dealt with in the matter of an innocent friendship with a boy, but the girl in question does not look back on the school with anything other than affection. Old Girls have been quite critical of the ordinariness of the curriculum, the mediocrity of some of the teaching, the unquestioning indoctrination in matters of religion and, to a modern mind, a quite disturbing inability or refusal to prepare girls for adolescence and some aspects of adulthood. I am sure that matters were not much different in other convent schools. The essential change since the 1960s is the diminution of the part played by the IBVM in the life of the school.

Sister Mark's was the last vocation into the Institute from the school. Discussion with present senior students has already been referred to, in which many willingly accept that "freely they have received and freely should give", and that they want to find ways of living useful Catholic Christian lives, recognising how many forms these may take in modern society. When I asked Sister Mark the question "Why are there no vocations to the IBVM now?" her view was that there are, but not in the West. In Korea, India and increasingly in Eastern Europe there are so many novices and juniors that the West will soon be outnumbered. This is not unique to the IBVM, but she did point out that she could name at least five Ascot Old Girls who have joined other congregations in this country over the last five years. This is due, she thinks, to the lack of clarity in the IBVM as to what it should be doing. "Who would wish to make a life-long commitment to an organisation with such unfocused aims?" She pointed out that many young people today find the thought of any kind of life commitment difficult whatever they choose—marriage or a religious vocation; after all, one out of three first marriages ends in the divorce courts in this country and more and more people are not getting married at all, and their relationships are not any more likely to be permanent. Furthermore, there are so many more openings for young women than there were thirty years ago. They grow up in a culture expecting them and encouraging them to go for good qualifications and a high-profile job. There are also many "vocational" jobs for the laity that were not possible thirty years ago; even spiritual direction is open to the laity. In many ways the laity can be more flexible than the Religious, not so burdened with inherited wealth, as many religious communities are, or with the problems of ageing communities very set in their ways. Then comes a characteristic Sister Mark (and Western European) comment:

The Church is so male-dominated that it deters the educated woman from seeking to serve it in religious life. Who are the women in the Vatican?—those who look after the material needs of the Catholic hierarchy. Hardly a place for the Sarah Hoggs of this world. To join religious life at this moment means taking a step backwards into a more restrictive and circumscribed existence. Mary Ward would have found this difficult too.

The stamp put on the school by the success of Sister Mark will not wear off. Her years in office have been remarkable; she has gone from narrowness of experience and unpreparedness for responsibility to clear, firm, and occasionally steely, command. She is an outstanding head by any standards and certainly so in the Catholic educational world, where there are so many problems and challenges, and a comparative dearth of highly talented people willing to take on positions of major responsibility. It was noticed earlier that there is a lack of Catholic applicants of quality for key posts in the school. Catholic laity and Religious are caught in tensions between the teachings of the Church and the needs and facilities of the modern world.

Transitions always bring great problems. There have been forces in the IBVM that would have withdrawn all its Sisters from teaching in Ascot, leaving only the presence at Errollston. Such a move was seen as the only entirely realistic one by those who advanced it: that the Sisters should disengage from teaching the daughters of the wealthy and privileged. They claimed that potential novices would not be attracted to this as their vocation. The governors resisted this view, realising that in Sister Mark, even in her early days, they had a remarkable head. But their very success, not achieved easily, left the slender IBVM presence a target for criticism. The head, unavoidably lonely, is sometimes seen as being in an invidious position, as a nun with power, in charge, and working in the world. The critics have wondered if *this* is a "role model" for vocations. Defenders, of whom I am emphatically one, would say that a Religious of her ability in this position, could not have acted otherwise, that she was put into headship by her superiors, with little help or support. She was acting under obedience, but the question must be put: why should not a nun, a woman, a woman in religion, occupy successfully a prominent and responsible position? Mary Ward said: "Vain fear and inordinate love are the bane of the female sex". (I can remember that an Ursuline nun was appointed to H.M. Inspectorate, with the approval of her Order and to the delight of the Senior Chief Inspector; in the event, she took up another position of responsibility.) It has been fortunate that Sister Mark has had the devoted service of her secretary, and of the bursar, and the consistent confidence of the governors.

The Bishops' Conference of England and Wales put out, in 1988, a document called "Evaluating the Distinctive Nature of a Catholic School". It was addressed first and foremost to the national provision of Voluntary-Aided Schools, but it is a worthwhile exercise to look at St Mary's against the Bishops' statement and its criteria. They point out that education does not take place only on a formal didactic basis, that the wider experiences on psychological, social, emotional and intuitive levels are also creative and, in many respects more important areas of learning. It is in these areas that values, attitudes and personal skills are required.

> The curriculum must reflect the fact that Christ is the foundation of the whole educational enterprise in a Catholic school. It may be convenient to speak of the religious curriculum and the secular curriculum, but in reality the curriculum as a whole and every part of it, is religious. For a school to be truly Catholic, this vision must be shared by all connected with its work. Everyone—teacher, pupil, governor, parent, other members of staff, priest or visitor—is on a personal journey of faith, and each person's stage on the journey is different.

This lengthy document insists that every aspect of the life of a Catholic school should be, so to speak, suffused by Catholic thought and emotion. This is a point that I have pursued often in my time, when I had a strong sense that everything in a school that I happened to be visiting, was the same as it would have been anywhere else, except that the RE was Catholic. There was a memorable occasion when a rather hostile senior civil servant asked the

Principal of a Catholic Institute of Higher Education: "What is different about this place from any other except that there is a crucifix on every wall ?" The Principal was angry, but it was a perfectly fair question.

How would this document be seen at Ascot? How much can be known about the spiritual or devotional life of the girls? Is it possible to assess the quality of the school as a Catholic school? Only the most tentative answers can be given based on talking with certain members of the teaching and pastoral staff and with some girls. The Chapel and the Sacraments remain central to the life of the school, though girls are no longer required to go to Mass every day, or Benediction three times a week, and one no longer gets the feeling, conveyed so strongly in past issues of the magazine, that a plenitude of religious feasts and festivals dominates the whole life of the school. Every morning does begin with school prayers, attendance is voluntary at any week-day Mass except Holy Days of Obligation, confessions are heard regularly—the minimum duty of the resident Chaplain is to say Mass and to hear confessions. Only in the last two years has there been a resident Chaplain, and I think that it is fair comment that his role was not thought through enough; it is unlikely that such a priest will be a trained teacher, and therefore, any of his work with classes or groups needs to take account of this. Religious Education is a compulsory subject for all girls in the GCSE examination. The school has not tied itself to any of the current national approaches, and certainly not to that particular scheme, known as "Weaving the Web", used in a large number of Catholic schools, but also a subject of great controversy because, to many, it is relativist in its thinking and methodology, and does not concentrate on the uniqueness of the Catholic Faith. The Head of Religious Education is a layman who feels strongly that all the girls should be properly instructed in Faith and Doctrine, should be familiar with the liturgical year, and that there should be proper attention given to Scripture, not least to the Old Testament. He is also responsible for organising Retreats, and other times of formal prayer. It is seen to be a strength that the teaching is mainly by lay people; girls are apt to take the line "Well she would say that wouldn't she?" of a point of view taken by a Sister. It may be recalled that some senior girls wanted more instruction in the teaching of the Church than they thought they were getting.

Eucharistic ministers are chosen from the girls; some are reluctant "volunteers". Some adults and, interestingly, some girls feel uncomfortable in receiving the Sacrament from pupils. There is not the same world of solemnities and processions that there once was. Sodalities faded out in the 1970s, but there is an impressive programme of Community Service and other good works carried out by the girls, and the sums of money collected for charity are startling—£20,000 to £30,000 in a year. The girls do not accept unquestioningly what they receive as the Church's teaching, and nor should they; gone are the days recalled by Old Girls when one listened, wrote it down, and never discussed. The more senior girls give every appearance of being independently minded, and at ease in their social world. I have no accurate means of knowing what proportion continues within the pattern of Catholic worship after they leave school. Girls and staff seem reasonably certain that a fairly large number of the girls keeps the Faith—against some odds, including belonging to families that themselves are divided or lapsed or indifferent in observance. If their Faith may not be much challenged at school, then it will certainly be challenged when they go, as most of them do, into higher education, where the current will flow against them. It may well be that then, the pattern will be what it now is for many others, a falling off, a lapsing to return later, a lapsing never to return.

Ascot can contribute, and give evidence to the national discussion about the purposes of the Catholic school. St Mary's is a firm example so far of a Faith being lived by a community within a community. The old days of no public questioning, of strict observance have passed. In other places I have argued that the Catholic school is a main means of preserving and developing identity. Others, I find, now feel that the most that we can do is to offer a particular kind of educational service. Discussion of this nature will intensify as the time of the IBVM withdrawal comes nearer. A very large "bank account" of spiritual living and example has been built up and drawn on for generations. Bank accounts do not last for ever without replenishing.

Personal and Social Education is not the same thing as Religious Education, and involves many more staff. I am told that about half of the teaching staff is not Catholic though most would certainly describe themselves as Christian. If there is a vacant teaching post, do you appoint the best-qualified applicant, or a runner-up who is Catholic or at least Christian? When an instance occurs in class, in any subject, where the teaching of the Catholic Church is different from that of other denominations, the matter is referred to the Catholic staff.

Now that Sister Gillian has taken up her post as IBVM Chaplain, girls with particular personal problems tend to be put into her care, and this is seen to be fruitful. She rightly sees her appointment as "Chaplain in General to the IBVM Schools" as a timely, perhaps overdue move to find a way of bringing back the spirit of Mary Ward and "the Ascot of the Nuns" into the present, much-changed situation. Her brief is to work mainly with the staff, parents and all other adults who are concerned and involved not just with the day-to-day running of the schools, but in their future as Catholic schools for girls, and as training grounds for Christian women committed to the Church and to values frequently at odds with those of the world. She writes that, since September 1992, she has directed the following activities:

1. September 1992, conference for all the school's staff: "The Distinctive Nature of the Catholic School".

2. Two workshops on ecumenism, requested by the non-Catholic staff: about thirty participated.

3. Small meetings for staff during Lent 1993, meeting three or four times a week, for prayer, discussion, Bible study, silence, or whatever else they wanted.

4. Two voluntary workshops on prayer—about fifteen participated.

5. Projects for the Autumn Term 1993: A day for parents and a day
for staff (and also, and not before time, for governors).

She sees her first concern to be for the quality of the spiritual life of
the school, and then to help to put personal Faith into corporate
Christian practice, and thirdly to explore how Christianity can per-
colate the whole of education. She wants to help the teaching staff
to feel competent in the pastoral care of the girls, to get away from
thinking that some questions are to be dealt with by Religious only.
"Perhaps I am trying to help implement the Church's stated aim of
helping the laity to reach spiritual adulthood and to accept responsibility for creating the Kingdom."

The school buildings themselves are no longer an ally. They represent the time when there was a single small community of girls
and Sisters, and no-one could fall through the net. Now they are
intractable. Whilst a girl will belong to the same House throughout
her schooling, and will be cared for within it and develop loyalties
which will find expression, for example, in games, the buildings dic-
tate that they sleep by the year, and therefore they develop other
loyalties; the task of the House mistresses is made that much more
difficult. There is then, no simple system of self-standing Houses as
in most boys' boarding schools. It seems likely that the youngest
receive the closest and most comforting attention, and that the middle years of adolescence can be as troublesome here as anywhere
else. The senior girls see the Mary Ward Courtyard as highly attractive and liberating, a powerful incentive to stay on after sixteen.
All this put together makes for a difficult pastoral system to run;
communication and coordination require continuous watchful-
ness. Here as elsewhere, not all senior girls combine freedom with
responsibility, and choosing and appointing staff on the pastoral
side is perhaps the most crucial responsibility to fall on the Head. As
with all communities, there is bullying, "borrowing", and plain
theft, and some girls, conscious of their monied background, can be

insolent and ill-mannered to people in whose care they are. These comments have been made to me by responsible people who are in authority; they have never been part of my experience in the school, and I know how much time and thought the staff give to the problems they encounter.

Rhian Amery thinks that the diminished IBVM presence has brought a serious challenge to the school's boarding life. To attract residential staff of the proper quality, very acceptable accommodation has had to be provided; flats for Housemothers have been "carved out" of the children's own sleeping area, and new houses built in the grounds for the five senior women who, as heads of House and deputy headmistress, are to become the cornerstones of the residential and pastoral life of the school. Houses for the headmistress and bursar, proper accommodation for the warden and assistant of the Mary Ward Courtyard, the adaptation of Gilmuire House to create nine flats for key residential staff, all these together have safeguarded the boarding life of the school. So now a growing number of staff lives on site, and the presence of staff families, adults and children has brought a new richness to communal life.

The school has attained an extraordinarily high academic reputation, which must reflect the teaching abilities of the staff. All heads of departments are lay. The pressures to maintain, and even to improve on this reputation are considerable. Rhian Amery emphasises how ways of monitoring closely and accurately each pupil's progress have been developed. From this came a new tutorial system, the introduction of regular assessments and the keeping of records of achievement; the involving of pupils in monitoring their own performance and setting their own academic targets has brought about a changed relationship between staff and pupils. Every member of the teaching staff enjoys, if that is the right word, an extended annual appraisal—with head of department, with deputy headmistress and headmistress. The academic curriculum has been broadened and developed—technology and computing for the younger pupils, for example, Economics, Politics, Classical Civilisation, History of Art and Theatre Studies at A Level. To this, programmes in life skills, community service, work experience, careers education, general studies, Duke of Edinburgh's Award Schemes have been added. She has written

> Evidence of success is easy to find. There is very keen competition for boarding places, and academic results are outstandingly good. In 1993 there was a 100% pass rate at A Level, of which 65% were A or B Grades; there was a 99% pass rate at GCSE, 81% at A or B Grades. In 1991, 1992 and 1993 almost all the girls went on to university, though many first took a "Gap Year".

The "work ethic" would delight the strictest Calvinist. There is a very great deal of teaching—by which I mean transmitting information. Some have said this amounts to over-teaching. Fitting this into all the other activities of the school creates problems and tensions; every area in the school wishes to shine, and each requires time, and more time. The remarkable growth in instrumental teaching in music, or the development of the Campion Singers would illustrate this point—music usually does.

Sister Mark, early in her headship, began a programme of colloquia for the whole staff and then for groups of staff teaching related subjects, to explain, first of all, the claims, the structure and the ethos of the Catholic Church. This prepared the way for Sister Gillian's work, and goes a long way to meeting the matters raised by the Bishops in 1988. Whether members of staff are Catholic or not, they have to be in general sympathy with the school, or else they would be personally unhappy. One such teacher says that she feels "comfortable" in St Mary's, and appreciates that no confessional approach is ever pushed. Should one pause and think about this? There is, as far as I can gather, no policy of introducing a Catholic point of view into, for example, the teaching of the Sciences. Straight explanations are given, and as I have already indicated, any ethical question arising is reserved to the Religious Education Department. This is fair enough in the circumstances. I do not see it like this in my own subject, History. I should be decid-

edly taken aback if Catholic interpretations of major areas of controversy were not put alongside others. If anyone wonders what I
mean, let me take you back to Chapter Two. What did happen to
the Church in England between 1535 and 1570? Is there "continuity";
is there a major fracture? Is the Church of England in direct continuity with the medieval "Ecclesia Anglicana", or is this not the case?
Where do Mary Ward and the recusant world fit in to History
teaching—a brief mention, or a careful exploration? The Head of
Religious Education has told me that six years ago, meetings were
held to examine where the Catholic point of view could reasonably
and sensibly be made part of subject teaching. All this needs fine-
tuning. One could become a tremendous bore. Pupils could be
"turned off" very successfully by a curriculum and teaching methods that over-emphasised Catholicism. The values that the school
teaches are often in tension with those of the world. Its pupils, like
Catholics everywhere, may find themselves in the divorce courts,
tempted to take drugs, commit offences that are punishable by law;
they will not fail to notice the differences between the Church's
teaching and some people's practice.

The Secretary of State for Education has now published his own
document on Spiritual and Moral Education which has been sent to
every school in England including the independent schools. It says
that "The Education Reform Act 1988, requires Her Majesty's Chief
Inspector of Schools to keep the Secretary of State informed about
the spiritual, moral, social and cultural development of all pupils."
These matters are to be "inspected". So much has the framework of
English education changed since 1983. Then, it would have been
unthinkable for a Cabinet Minister to write, and to write so direct-
ively, to schools. When I advanced such views, between 1977 and
1984, I ran into argument and worse in many schools and with some
of my colleagues, especially about the definition of the word "spiritual". The Secretary of State now lays it down that school leavers
should be able to :

Distinguish between right and wrong

Articulate their attitudes and values
Take responsibility for their own actions
Recognise the spiritual and moral dimension to situations
Understand the long- and short-term consequences of their
actions for themselves and others
Behave consistently in accordance with their principles

and much else. Inspectors are to be required to establish whether a
school has a consistent and agreed approach to the ways in which
spiritual and moral issues should be addressed throughout the
school; whether it promotes an ethos which values imagination,
inspiration, contemplation, and a clear understanding of right and
wrong. All that I can say is that many schools and teachers are going
to be mightily perplexed by all this, but St Mary's should not be one
of them.

Having studied and sought out the IBVM from its beginnings at
Ascot in 1885, I find it a moving experience to walk down to the
cemetery where so many of these Sisters are buried, "in sure and
certain hope of Resurrection". There they lie, so dedicated in their
lives, so sure in their vocations, the ones who taught and the ones
who kept the boilers, ran the laundry or cultivated the garden and
milked the cows, still gathered around Mother Cecilia. Mother
Joseph Edwards and the other pioneers are there, certainly, but
Mother Cecilia is *the* presence. The "undying" community is here,
the graveyard as immaculately kept as they kept the school in their
lifetime. It is wonderfully quiet, rather hidden away. They were a
compact sisterhood, almost everyone of whom would have known
where her last resting place was to be. Not far away, the sounds of
the living school can be heard. I have rarely had so strong a sense of
"eternal rest". But the school is not the school as it used to be. Of the
twelve governors, three are members of the IBVM. In a large teaching, administrative, managerial, medical, indoors and outdoors
staff, only six are IBVM, other than Sister Mark herself. This year
there have been 40 students in the Upper Sixth, 44 in the Lower

Sixth, 43 in the Upper Fifth. Entry into the school is over-subscribed. Achievements in external examinations are outstandingly good, and the tide of recipients of prizes and cups at Prize Day may begin to seem unstoppable and unending.

Recent school magazines, in their lists of marriages and Old Girls' careers, shew clearly that the goals of past times are by no means dead, though there is the sticking point of no vocations into the IBVM itself. "To set the world on fire with the love of God"—Mary Ward's own purpose in her work with girls—may now seem dramatic, even melodramatic language to many modern pupils, though Sister Mark has proclaimed this still to be the ultimate purpose of the school. Notions of service to God, in very different ways, without doubt flourish in the minds of past and present pupils.

Cecilia Marshall, Ignatius Beveridge, Bridget Geoffrey-Smith, Mark Orchard: there is no escaping the succession. So far, so good; but this either looks to a future of continuing success along present lines, or else it reminds one that this same comment was made by the man who threw himself from the top of the Empire State Building, when he was two-thirds of the way down.

There are such big question marks. The future of boarding itself is uncertain; weekly boarding is the drift, and the number of day places increases—parents who are finding full boarding fees more and more difficult to meet can afford day fees. The governors of St Mary's give considerable time to discussing how to expand the bursary scheme, and other ways of helping parents in trouble—but this requires the building up of a very large capital sum. Many are now questioning the idea itself of an exclusively Catholic school; some of the major boys' Catholic schools are finding the going very hard. Geographical position has acquired a new importance: Ascot is, at any rate, well-placed in this matter. The school is attractive enough now to hold on to senior girls, post-sixteen, though it has been put to me, pretty strongly, that there are not enough facilities and spaces even now, in which senior girls can be with their boy friends. So, can St Mary's be afforded, is it worth affording, will it be able to continue, as it now is, as a very successful single-sex "all through" girls' school, a Catholic girls' school? I have assumed all along, and certainly never discussed it with Sister Mark, that Ascot is and always will be a single-sex girls' school. Is this axiomatic? Boys' schools are admitting girls. Should girls' schools admit boys? Would they come, would they stay, and what would it do to the nature of the school? The evidence from Oxford and Cambridge women's colleges that have introduced men is not encouraging. Equality, in anything, does not seem to have been achieved.

I am feeling my way to a larger question, about young people today—well-to-do young people—their parental circumstances, their views about contemporary behaviour patterns, values and career opportunities, as against the teaching of the Church, and the values it holds, many of which contradict those of society. In conversation, I have been told that many of the senior girls are not as sophisticated as they think they are, and that their knowledge and understanding of worlds beyond their own are decidedly limited; their travels, which may be extensive, tend to keep them within their own boundaries. The Gap Year may well take them to Peru, but perhaps they should know more about Bootle; there is a Third World here. I am not playing down all the good works that are done locally, but rather asking questions. Rhian Amery recalls that an Old Girl, distinguished at Cambridge and at the LSE, helped to found a charity to help educate Ugandan children orphaned by the Aids epidemic. The cost for one child for one year is twenty pounds, and a Sixth Form girl pondered on this as against Ascot fees. It is a fair pondering on an unsound comparison, but it shews that worries about the school for the "daughters of the rich" continue, and I hope that properly informed discussions do as well.

One comes back to the girls themselves. What do they make of it by the time they reach the Sixth Form? In general many of their thoughts are similar to those of girls who have gone before them all the way back over a hundred years and more—gratitude for knowing the liturgical year, the practice of the Rosary, some knowledge of the life and achievements of Mary Ward, and the easiness and naturalness of going into Chapel whenever they wish. There is the continuing emphasis on sense of community, of growing through the developments of one's own talents, of increasing independence as one grows older, and now the warmth and comfort of the Mary Ward Courtyard. A note of caution is sounded: "It's a weird situation to be in, three hundred and sixty girls all from roughly the same background, all there to do approximately the same things. It helps you to appreciate the smaller qualities that build a person's individuality. You'd get really bored if you didn't." Finally there is the pointed remark: "Undoubtedly we are aware of being a closeted community, very much removed from society. We are told to prepare for 'real life' but discouraged from experiencing it. This of course creates a sense of frustration amongst those of us who feel that the two should at least in part go hand in hand." I could remark ironically that if one were to tease out an agreed statement on the characteristics of "real life", then God help the school that gives its pupils experience of it.

One is setting the most extraordinarily difficult task to the staff of a school, at one and the same time to continue successfully what they are doing now, and yet to give considered and systematic thought to the patterns and new structures which the future will demand. There is no comfort in the only memorable, and truly unarguable statement by former President Nixon that "the future, my friends, the future lies ahead".

In 1993, the European Union came into being. Freedom of movement, freedom to seek work, a determination to arrive at a complete equivalence in all qualifications within a community of three hundred and forty million people, signalled the opening up of a new kind of society for all its members, with consequences at present not always grasped by young people who will be in their mid-twenties by the end of the century. Sister Mark appreciated this development early, and moved into equipping the school to face it, not only in her own visits to Brussels and elsewhere, but in appointing the European coordinator. It may be that there there is not yet full exploitation of these opportunities, in, for example, links with

Continental institutions. There is a European Catholic culture, alive and well, with a marked emphasis toward young people, with which the school should be much more involved. The European Catholic vision is exciting and challenging. One million young Catholics, by no means all Polish, went to meet the Pope at Poland's national shrine; many had walked for days to get there. There is an immense store of idealism, energy and love to be tapped in the European Catholic young, and we have barely begun to do so. I can foresee the exasperated reaction of many, certainly on the teaching staff, on reading this. What? All this in addition to ten or twelve subjects at GCSE and four at A Level, making for an even more crowded day? Somehow or other, those who run and work in schools are going to have to take sufficient time off, to think in an uncluttered way about the likely future. This, after all, has been one of the purposes of Sister Mark's sabbatical year.

Sir Christopher Ball, in address given at Bedales School during its centenary celebrations in June 1993 said:

> Perhaps the best test of a school's success and vitality is its ability to renew itself, to redefine its role, and face the challenge of change and prepare for an uncertain future. We are the first people in history who have known for sure that they do not know what the future will be like. The only thing that we can be certain of is that it will be different. Our predecessors thought that the future would be like the present and the recent past, so they provided an education based on the best of the past, on the assumption that it would provide the best for the future . . . I fear that my (and your) great-grandchildren will accuse us of some carelessness in the way we raise our young and develop the full potential in our society. And they will be right.

St Mary's Ascot is, in many and fundamental ways, different from Bedales. Nevertheless, those who guide it cannot escape the challenge that Sir Christopher put down. The coming years will bring opportunities and trials, some foreseen and others unpredictable.

The search for Sister Mark's successor, in order to hand over to the laity, should begin soon. The most that she and the governors can work for is to pass on the school faithful to its origins and fully equipped to meet all likely academic developments. What cannot be planned for is political and social change. This book started with a defence of independent schools and the rights of parents to choose them. What I think is irrefutable is not seen to be so by many others, and a political change of government could bring unfriendly legislation. Within the independent schools, there is already noticeable a trend away from boarding; if this became so at Ascot, there would have to be a far-reaching review of the use of its buildings. We are not helped by the fact that within the Church in this country, amongst clergy, Religious and laity, there is a foggy and often not well-informed drifting argument about the desirability of the confessional school at all. Some see it as "divisive". Firm and clear leadership will be needed to pilot St Mary's through these rocks and shallows. Change must not bring loss of its inherited and valued identity.

Mary Ward said in the Third Verity Talk towards the end of November 1617:

It is good for you to think in (all) these occasions: *Anima justi in manu Dei est.* The souls of (all) the just are in the hands of God. Indeed it will be best for you to think that howsoever others seem to be to you, it is best for you to think that God does rule and govern the just and that all things are wrought for our good.

All this, I assure you is truth; the cause I have spoken is not to excuse myself in anything, or desire any of your esteem, for my eyes are fixed on another object. This is all for the present . . . I desire to make you know and love Verity . . . So God bless you all.

The Painted Life of Mary Ward and her First Companions, with Particular Reference to the Twenty-Second Painting

Sister Gillian Orchard IBVM gave most of the information in this appendix.

The Painted Life of Mary Ward is a record of what holiness meant for her and, by extension, for her Institute, and those who are in any way attracted by her charisma. She was determined to achieve a complete freedom from all that can make one cling to created things, and completely to dedicate herself and her Sisters to a life of openness to all good works.

The Painted Life, therefore, is not just a memorial to a great woman, a seventeenth-century version of the family photograph album, at which one looks and remembers "the good things past"; its focus is more truly towards the future, because it enshrines in its visual images the spiritual will and testament of a person whose life was entirely given to her Creator, who was in her own words "satisfied with nothing less than God". The message is enduring and springs out of the picture frame.

The present fifty (originally fifty-one) pictures portray selected scenes and incidents from Mary Ward's life. They hang in a specially-built gallery opened in 1977 in the IBVM house in Augsburg, which is the longest-enduring house of the Institute. They have not always had such a sympathetic home, indeed, like the foundress, they have travelled, and even suffered temporary oblivion. The paintings are by several artists, and date from the second half of the seventeenth century. Mary Poyntz, one of the earliest friends and member of the original group around Mary Ward, was the foundress of the Augsburg Community and it was she, along with Winifred Wigmore, who wrote Mary Ward's first biography. They commissioned many of the pictures, though which is not known.

They are known to have been displayed in the Paradeiser House in Munich from 1680 to 1717. They were then removed to the Augsburg house. There arose a considerable controversy over jurisdiction, a rivalry between St Polten in Austria and the Houses of Bavaria, which was fanned by the attempts to extend her Imperial powers by the Austrian Empress Maria Theresa. The situation was aggravated by Pope Benedict XIV's Bull of 1749, *Quamvis Iusto*, which continued the papal policy of approving the Institute of Mary but denying the title of Foundress to Mary Ward. It was during this time that a local ecclesiastical chapter, in high dudgeon, declared that "More than thirty paintings portraying visions, revelations, ecstasies, and apparitions of this kind, all unfounded, are displayed for all to see. They should be completely banished." The pictures were an embarrassing witness to the holiness of a person whose name it was hoped would be obliterated from the memory of the Church and the Institute. The paintings were removed—for a time—but it is recorded in the Augsburg chronicle that on the anniversary of Mary Ward's death, January 30th 1773, "the paintings of her life were hung up". And there they remained for another sixty years till another bishop vented his disapproval, as a result of which the canvases were rolled up and relegated to the attic.

That they ever saw the light of day again is due in no small measure to the interest shewn by two English Jesuits towards the end of the nineteenth century. Frs Henry Coleridge and John Morris inspired the Sisters in England with the confidence to reclaim their Foundress and their spiritual inheritance: Fr Coleridge by supporting the production of the first definitive life of Mary Ward by Mother Catherine Chambers in 1885; Fr John Morris in his work of bringing the Painted Life to the forefront of the Institute's consciousness again. During a visit to Augsburg in 1889, he wrote to Mother Loyola Giles at the Bar Convent in York that "I have spent a couple of hours over the Painted Life today, of which the Bishop spoke to me. There are forty-six pictures—there were fifty-two in Fridl's time, and in a very bad condition, but the whole in a far better order than one could have expected. The Reverend Mother here is going to have them framed, backed, and cleaned and varnished. How I should like to get them all!" Four years later, Fr John Morris became the proud owner of the first photographic reproduction of the fifty pictures that survive today.

The ravages of the Second World War left their mark on Augsburg. The House was destroyed by fire, but fortunately the pictures were saved by the foresight of Mother Aloysia Löffler, who organised their removal to a castle of the Fugger family. Now, in the 1990s, after a chequered three hundred years' existence, they hang in safety and have become a source of inspiration to many.

A caption in German describing the subject matter was added at a later date to each painting. The round brackets in the list below indicate where these captions have been paraphrased. The paintings reproduced in colour in this book, nos. 4, 9, 13, 14, 21, 22, 27, 30, have more information about them, in square brackets.

1. The first word that Mary uttered was Jesus, after which she did not speak again for several months.

2. In the tenth year of her age, Mary was urged by her parents to marry . . . She prayed fervently to God imploring Him to prevent this marriage . . . Her prayers were heard.

3. In the tenth year of her age, Mary had such a serious fall that she lost the power of speech. She thought within her self: "Oh, how gladly would I die if only I could once say the saving Name of Jesus." As she pronounced it she became quite well again . . .

4. In the year 1595, when Mary was in her eleventh year . . . a great fire broke out at her father's mansion at Mulwith. She was not alarmed,

but remained in a room saying the Rosary with her sisters until their father came to rescue them. [Mary's autobiographical notes give a fuller version of events. "I was caught in the thick of it, very aware of the danger, and I besought Our Lady to extinguish the flames, or at least to save us all. I then seized two younger sisters (both of whom happily lived to survive and die in our Institute), dragged them into a lower room where there was a large chest filled with linen and damask (my trousseau, people said). The three of us heaved the chest into the chimney breast and settled ourselves behind it to pray the Mother of God for deliverance, never for a moment doubting that she would do so. And by God's providence, my father suddenly missed us and because he loved us more than life or limb, plunged back into the burning building and led us out to safety."]

5. When Mary was in her twelfth year, she was again urged by her parents to marry . . . She insisted on refusing, esteeming that God alone was worthy of her love.

6. When Mary was thirteen (she was tempted by the devil to put off first communion).

7. In her thirteenth year . . . Mary prepared with great zeal and devotion for her first communion.

8. When Mary was in her thirteenth year, (on account of threatening persecution) she was sent to stay with a relative (and again urged to marry. Her father fetched her home.)

9. When Mary was fifteen, she sat sewing with her cousin Barbara Babthorpe. (She was told of persecution and punishments, and resolved to enter the religious life.) [From Mary's autobiographical notes; the scene is the Babthorpe family home of Osgodby, near Selby in Yorkshire and the storyteller was an old maid-servant called Margaret Garrett. "Once, as we sat sewing together in the same room, she told a story of a nun who had violated her vow of

chastity and had become pregnant. Punishment dictated that she be subject to the strictest seclusion for several years and that she lie prostrate at the door of the convent chapel, so that her sisters on passing in and out might tread on her. This monstrous penance magnified the offence, it seemed to me. Similar occurrences were neither rare, nor very disgraceful, nor so severely punished among ordinary folk in the world. At which point I immediately conceived an extraordinary love and respect for the religious state, a sacred place where holiness was the be-all and end-all."]

10. When Mary was sixteen and read the lives of the holy martyrs, (she became determined to follow them, but our Saviour revealed to her . . . that what He required of her was spiritual rather than bodily martyrdom).

11. God revealed to her that the martyrdom that He expected of her was the perfect observance of the religious state.

12. When Mary was twenty (all her friends, secular and religious, tried to dissuade her from entering the religious life. She prayed for God's assistance in resisting them.)

13. In 1606, Mary was urged by parents and priests to marry (the sole heir of the Nevilles, a powerful ancient North Country family. She resisted.) [Edmund Neville, heir to the Earl of Westmorland, had proposed to her. Her parents and her confessor, Fr Richard Holtby, could not persuade her. "I felt some distress but suddenly the words of the Gospel came to mind: 'Seek ye first the kingdom of God' (Luke 12, 31). The burden was lifted and I was immediately sure that if I cooperated in embracing the 'better part' and preferring the honour and service of God to all else, he in his generosity would supply what I lacked. These same words have stood me in good stead at other times when things seem to be impossible."]

14. (When staying in London in 1606, an incident at Mass made the

priest promise to further her in every way in the religious life.) [Fr Holtby spilled the chalice, which he took as a sign, and afterwards, as he dried his hands on a towel he was moved to declare that he would no longer stand in opposition.]

15. (Mary took ship to St Omer after Whitsuntide 1606, to enter the Religious state.)

16. (In 1609, Mary made a vow to return to England to work for the salvation of souls.)

17. (Mary brought about the conversion of a very wealthy but obstinate lady, after everyone else had failed to do so. The lady died a pious Catholic.)

18. (Her desire to make converts led her to dress as a serving maid, the better to approach those she wished to bring to the Faith.)

19. (Mary persuaded a Jesuit to try to bring her aunt to the true Faith.)

20. When Mary was in London, a noble gentleman sent his servants to her with a fine collation of dainty food. (Mary feared that this was a temptation from the devil.) So she locked herself in her room and spent the night in prayer and penance.

21. (In 1609, Mary fell into an ecstasy.) While in this state, she perceived clearly that it was not God's will for her to enter an austere order, but she was called to a much more excellent state . . . After a space of two hours . . . a long time elapsed before she could hear anything except the word GLORY. [Mary had left the Poor Clare community in St Omer where she had been a novice. The experience described here is known in the IBVM tradition as the "Glory vision". "One morning while meditating rather half-heartedly and not at all to my satisfaction, I made a resolution at the close to assist a person

who wanted to become a nun, but who had no dowry and therefore could not enter. I dressed according to the fashion of the day, and while I was arranging my hair in front of the mirror, something very supernatural happened to me ... I was shewn with great clarity an indescribable certainty that I was not to be an enclosed nun but that some other destiny was ordained for me ... I did not see what this assured good thing would be, but the glory of God, which it portended, shewed itself in such a way I cannot explain but nevertheless so overwhelmingly that my whole being resounded with the words: GLORY, GLORY, GLORY ...".]

22. [This picture, of Mary Ward and her first companions, could be called the emblem of this book. It is described in more detail on page 183.]

23. (At St Omer, Mary feared that she might love her Confessor too much.) Then Christ appeared visibly to her and said, "Oh foolish child, it is not thou, but I who choose him for thee."

24. In 1611, as Mary, beginning to recover from a mortal illness, lay in bed at St Omer, all alone in an extraordinary repose of mind, she perceived quite plainly by an interior voice in what way she was to organise her Institute.

25. On the feast of All Saints in 1615, at St Omer, God shewed Mary a just soul in inexpressible beauty.

26. Mary was at sea on the feast of St James 1618, when she invoked this holy Apostle in order to quell a dangerous mutiny. (Mary claimed that she never vainly sought favours from God by invoking St James.)

27. When in London, Mary meditated on the words "AND THOU SHALT CALL HIS NAME JESUS". (She became convinced that all those who gave themselves selflessly to her work in the Institute

would achieve salvation.) [The picture links up with the spiritual exercises of St Ignatius at the start of the second Week, in which the retreatant is asked to imagine God the Father looking down on the earth and on the human race as it goes about its chaotic pattern of living. (Top left and middle left) Taking compassion on a lost people, God sends his Son (Nativity at Bethlehem top centre) to restore and reconcile the world to himself, including those who preceded Jesus, saints and heroes of the Old Testament (centre bottom). Those who chose to go their own way chose damnation (centre left).]

28. In 1618, Mary was grieving over her sins with many tears, when God clearly revealed that she was to make satisfaction for them in this life. (She asked God to shew her how this might be done and realised that her life would be filled with tribulation.)

29. (Mary prayed for a priest whom she had rescued from an evil life. God assured her that he would stay in a state of grace.)

30. In 1619, at St Omer, when Mary was fervently thanking God for the grace of her vocation, He shewed her clearly that to help to save souls is a far greater gift than the monastic life or even than martyr-dom itself. [Mary was working on the plan of her Institute to pre-sent to the Pope for approval. She wanted to take the Constitutions of the Society of Jesus, with adjustments for women, the chief thrust of which is mission, work for God among human beings of all kinds. Here Mary is considering the growth of her vocation to apostolic service. Not for her the martyrdom she dreamt of as a young girl (top left), not the traditional monastic Orders of the Church, which she had tried and found not to her satisfaction (top centre). *Her* field of activity was to be with ordinary people, the great multitude of men and women, saints and sinners, old and young, educated and unlettered, rich and poor, sick and in health (foreground).]

31. (Mary's perception that the Apostles lived in complete poverty

renewed in her a determination) to attain to perfect self-denial. Suddenly she experienced a feeling of complete liberty and detachment from earthly things.

32. (In 1619, Mary was disturbed that she was not being persecuted or suffering in some way for Christ. At Mass, He shewed her plainly that her distress was not pleasing to Him because it came from self-will.)

33. In 1619, at Liège, God shewed Mary how many souls would be lost and how few saved . . . Their free will alone had condemned them to burn in hell.

34. On October 10th 1619, (Mary, in retreat, became convinced that God would guide her and keep her).

35. In 1619 in the church of St Martin at Liège, before the crucifix near the sanctuary, God revealed to Mary that although the Institute was not to be altogether subject to the Society of Jesus, yet it ought to be under its direction, in order to preserve and not to deviate from its true spirit.

36. (Mary's prayers brought about a complete recovery from illness of Cardinal Trescio, after her pilgrimage to a shrine of Our Lady.)

37. (In 1625, God revealed to Mary during a journey the glory of life in the religious state.)

38. (God made known to Mary in Rome that her Institute would prosper and succeed only if its members depended entirely on Him.)

39. In 1625, in Rome, Mary heard an interior voice telling her that she would afford God the greatest pleasure if she bore her trials joyfully.

40. (Mary had a mystical experience on April 11th 1625.) The intense brilliancy of the rays of light proceeding from the Blessed Sacrament shone on her face and deprived her for a while of her sight.

41. (Mary, praying before the Blessed Sacrament, was enlightened by God regarding the forgiveness of enemies.) Henceforth she cherished a tender affection for all who wronged her and was in the habit of calling them friends and lovers of her heavenly reward.

42. (In 1626, God reminded Mary) of the adversities, persecutions and trials she would have to encounter in accomplishing His Holy Will.

43. On Christmas Eve 1626 Mary arrived at Feldkirch in Tyrol; in spite of her fatigue and the intense cold, she remained in church from eight o'clock in the evening until three in the morning, absorbed in prayer.

44. (Mary, at Mass on Christmas Day 1626 in Feldkirch, prayed for the conversion of the King of England. God agreed with her) but that the King's cooperation was wanting.

45. (God revealed to Mary, as she was travelling to Munich in 1626, that the Elector would house and take care of her and of her companions.)

46. In 1626, Mary was very sad because one of her companions was thinking of giving up her vocation. (God revealed to her that the Institute would be secured but in His own good time.)

47. (God told Mary that she was not to think about or worry concerning money to maintain the Institute.)

48. (Mary rescued a novice from disaffection and brought her peace) saying: "Dear child, virtue is hard only to those who consider

it to be so; your way to heaven must be to accept everything from God's hand, and to seek him alone".

49. (God revealed to Mary that a distinguished-looking man) unknown to her and dressed as a bishop . . . was a friend of her Institute.

50. At St Omer, God granted Mary a sight of great glory, saying to her: "Be not weary, you shall die soon, and your reward shall be great."

22. Mary Ward with her first companions in 1609
Mary Poyntz: 1593 to 1667

Opposite Mary Ward on the left of the picture is Mary Poyntz who, born in 1593, is the youngest in the group. She was the daughter of Edward and Mary Poyntz of Newark Park, an Elizabethan hunting lodge near Wotton-under-Edge in Gloucestershire, and elder sister of John Poyntz who became a Jesuit and was sent on the English mission in the 1620s. Mary Poyntz, like Mary Ward, resisted family pressure to accept marriage because she wanted to join this band of friends. She left her disappointed suitor with a portrait of herself: the left side of her face was her living likeness, the right side a death's head "and from the cheek down to the chest the flesh was quite corrupted and eaten by worms". The picture made such an impression on the young man that he too gave up worldly pursuits and entered a religious Order.

From 1609 to 1627 Mary Poyntz lived and worked alongside Mary Ward. She was with her in 1611 on the visit to Our Lady of Montaigue's shrine when the Foundress received clear direction as to the nature of her Institute: "Take the same of the Society". She certainly accompanied Mary Ward in her several journeys to England before 1621, and then to Rome to present the Third Plan of the Institute to Pope Gregory XV. For four years she taught in the schools in Rome and acted as secretary on official business. When the Roman schools were closed in 1625, Mary Ward decided to visit her distant communities in England and Flanders, and to go by way of Germany rather than France, via Bavaria, where the Elector and his wife received them with generosity. By January 1627, they had moved into the Paradeiser House in Munich, and Mary Poyntz was appointed the first superior of the community. Winifred Bedingfield was to be the Headmistress and Cecily Morgan the novice mistress. For the first time in their lives in the Institute, the two Marys were separated, but not for long.

Within a year Winifred Wigmore was called to support Mary Ward in Vienna, Pressburg and Prague, where there were great difficulties in setting up communities and schools that met the approval of the ecclesiastical and political authorities. The Bull of Suppression was promulgated in 1631. Mary Poyntz was present when it reached Munich, and the Dean solemnly read the indictment to Mary Ward (and Anne Turner). She went with them to the Poor Clare convent, installed Mary Ward in her "palace" as she was wont to call it, and kept her supplied with warm clothes carefully wrapped in brown paper; she also supplied the prisoner with lemon juice, and the two of them kept up a lively correspondence under the noses of the gaolers, with the help of a candle and good eyesight. Mary Poyntz not only looked to the material needs of an ailing friend but also organised an uninterrupted course of intercessory prayer and asked all the other communities to do the same. Within two months Mary Ward was released and determined to go to Rome to plead her innocence. Mary Poyntz did not go with her this time: money was very short, and her task was to keep the Munich school and community going as best she could. Two years later, ill and tired, she rejoined her friend in Rome, and was again put in charge of the community. Here she and other members lived under Papal supervision till the late 1630s when they first decided that nothing more was to be gained by staying. Mary Ward was a very sick woman by this time, and wanted to return to her native land. So Mary Poyntz handed the office of Superior in Rome to Barbara Babthorpe, and began the long and wearisome journey back to

England. From London the Civil War drove them north to York-shire, where they established a community in Heworth, just outside York. Mary Poyntz was present with Winifred Wigmore, Catherine Smith and Frances Bedingfield at the deathbed of Mary Ward on January 30th 1645.

Five years later the little community moved to Paris, where Mary Poyntz and Winifred Wigmore worked together on "A Briefe Rela-tion of the Holy Life and Happy Death of our Dearest Mother", the first biography of Mary Ward, and as yet unpublished.

In 1653, Mary Poyntz returned to Rome to take up the office of chief Superior in succession to Barbara Babthorpe who resigned on the grounds of ill-health, but she did not stay long there. She moved back to Bavaria where the Institute had received some sort of recog-nition from the ruling family, and from there she governed the Institute until 1662 when she was requested by the Elector to open a house in the Imperial city of Augsburg, which she did. She also undertook the training of the novices, in addition to her leadership of the company that she had seen grow, flourish, and decline—but not completely. She died on September 30th, 1667 suffering a stroke at the age of seventy-four, the longest-lived companion of that first 1609 circle. She is buried in St John's Churchyard in Munich, in an unmarked grave.

Jane Browne: 1581 to 1630

In the National Portrait Gallery there is an engraving of "concilium septem nobilium anglorum coniurantium", known to most of us as the Gunpowder Plotters. As with the Painted Life the artist remains unknown. The date is 1605, and each conspirator is named. Not only are they named but each one is connected in kinship. This fam-ily interconnectedness helps to place Jane (or Joanna) Browne in this company. Her mother was a sister of Lady Grace Babthorpe, also of the wife of Ambrose Rookwood. She was related to the Catesby family, yet another link between the engraving and this painting. She was a member of the Yorkshire recusant network.

She is seated second from the left, next to Mary Poyntz. At twenty-eight, she was the eldest of the group and brings to it an air of repose and sense of peacefulness. Her hands are at rest, her features tranquil, and she seems to be engaging our attention, and inviting us to share the lively discussion that may have been going on.

When her father died in 1614, Jane left St Omer and returned to England, where after settling family affairs, she joined Susanna Rookwood who is seated two places away on Jane's left, in the work that continued in London. She and Susanna formed a solid apostolic partnership: in 1623 they were both in Naples, Jane in charge of the children who came for schooling and Susanna in the office of Superior, though only briefly because she died there in 1624; Winifred Wigmore was appointed in her place. Jane then became "minister" and took on much of the day-to-day running of the house which became increasingly difficult as the community grew poorer and poorer. She suffered a long and painful illness which she endured in the troubled times when the schools were closed and the Institute suppressed in Naples in 1629, anticipating by a year or so the Bull of Suppression.

Jane was called to Munich by Mary Ward where she was cared for with the love and compassion that Mary herself always encouraged her sisters to shew towards the sick, wherever they were found. "What!" she is reputed to have exclaimed when one of the community ventured to comment on the "luxury" of Jane being given two rooms and a permanent attendant, "Would you that we should spare any expense for one who formerly never spared herself in the service of Jesus Christ?" Jane Browne died on February 23rd 1630 in Munich.

Catherine Smith: 1583 (?) to 1655

Mother Catherine Chambers, in her attempt to establish the family credentials of Catherine Smith, the third companion from the left, found it difficult to shew the connection with the rest of the group. There is much conjecture but little evidence. She joined the community because she shared their vision, not necessarily because she belonged to the "right" or the "same" social groups.

She was at St Omer in 1609, and visited England again with Mary Ward some time before 1621. Then she became Superior of one of the houses in Flanders, and was there in 1631 when the Bull of Suppression was issued, and all the houses were closed and the communities dispersed. She was one of the faithful few despite great "hunger and want" and made her way to Munich, which became the haven of the survivors of the suppression. From there she went to Rome to live on the Esquiline with the other members of the disbanded Institute. In the late 1630s she was part of the group that made a slow and painful journey back to England, first to London, then to Yorkshire. She was present when Mary Ward died. Five years later she was in Paris and died there on April 29th 1655. Sister Gillian has written that "From this 'thin' story, one might imagine that Catherine shrank from the limelight and enjoyed a cloak of invisibility. I think that the person in the picture belies that notion. Notice how Susanna Rookwood is laying a restraining hand on her arm. She was a woman of fire and energy, like the rest of them."

Susanna Rookwood: 1583 to 1624

Early in 1609 Mary Ward stayed at the Rookwood family home, Coldham Hall in Suffolk. It was a fruitful time. She was instrumental in bringing a dying woman back to the faith. She met with cousins and kin, and caught up with the news of what had happened as a result of the Gunpowder Plot in 1605 that had made life very hazardous for Catholics. She also spent time with Susanna, a young woman of twenty-six, and persuaded her to join in the venture she felt herself divinely called to. Susanna was immediately attracted by the enthusiasm and faith of her younger cousin. Like Mary, she felt the pull of "doing something for England". Her brother Ambrose had been sacrificed for the Catholic cause as a result of his involvement with the Gunpowder Plot.

Susanna sits at the centre of the circle in Plate number 22 of the

Painted Life. She probably features in Plate 17 as well, which depicts life at Coldham Hall. In 1609 she chose to go with Mary to St Omer, and there seek light on the meaning of this vocation to the apostolic life. Within a few years Susanna was in London as superior of a community of six members, leading the double life that Catholics were compelled to live in dangerous days. We are told that Susanna "was very often in danger of her life for the Catholic faith, to which she brought back a large number of souls, and preserved and strengthened many others. She was five times in prison for her religion, where she encouraged and refreshed the other prisoners both by spiritual and temporal means . . ."

By 1621 Susanna was in Liège, looking after Anne Gage, whose health was failing. The next year Mary Ward asked her to come to Rome to assist in the presentation and defence of the Third Plan of the Institute before the committee of cardinals. So for a year Susanna worked as a secretary and assistant to Mary Ward, who valued her services highly but realised that her spiritual gifts were under-used. Consequently, when the new house was set up in Naples in 1623, Susanna was named the first Superior. She was in office only six months when she became ill and died on May 25th 1624. Mary Poyntz and Winifred Wigmore remembered Susanna in their Briefe Relation some twenty years later. "She had an extraordinary zeal for the honour of God and the salvation of souls. At Naples, as superior of the house of the Institute there, she gave an incomparable example of love, wisdom and goodness, an especial love for spiritual things, as well as a perfect humility and greatness of soul, so that not only the community but also the people of the city were greatly edified by her." Susanna Rookwood was thus the first of this little group to die.

Winifred Wigmore: 1585 to 1657

Winifred Wigmore sits next to Mary Ward in this group. This is appropriate, because she can be seen to be the "beloved disciple" and confidante. She is seated in her scarlet dress listening carefully to her teacher. She was Mary Ward's closest and most intimate companion and received the greatest number of letters affectionately addressed to "Win".

The Wigmores came from Herefordshire. She was born in the same year as Mary, 1585, and she first met her at Coughton Court in Warwickshire, the home of the Throckmorton family of whom Anne Wigmore, Winifred's mother, was a member. That was most likely in 1605, as it was in that year that Mary Ward travelled from Yorkshire to the south coast to catch the boat to St Omer, with the intention of becoming an enclosed Religious. In 1609, they met again in London and Winifred joined the small group of women, a brave act because she herself was cautious, even timid by nature, and worried about the more daring exploits of the others.

Between 1614 and 1618 she made several journeys to England with Mary Ward, and in 1619 became novice mistress in one of the houses in Liège. This shy, modest woman travelled to Cologne, Trier and Brussels, and then endured the long journey to Rome with Mary Ward in 1621. Two years later, she went further south to become novice mistress in Naples, and so was separated from her leader for the longest time. The death of Susanna Rookwood, her Superior in Naples, made her the obvious successor, but she resisted the appointment fiercely and successfully.

At the suppression of the Institute Winifred moved to Munich where she allowed herself to be appointed "vice-rectrice" to support her cousin, Mary Poyntz. From there she went back to Liège to help the struggling community, and like Mary Ward, found herself confined and under arrest in 1631. She was released in April at the same time as Mary, and went with her to Rome to set up a community on the Esquiline. With Catherine Smith and Mary Poyntz, Winifred was one of the little band who returned to England, to be with her beloved friend at her death.

In 1650 she went to Paris with the Heworth community, became headmistress of the school, and novice mistress for the third time. She died in April 1657 at the age of seventy-two, and is buried in the convent cemetery of the Bernadine Sisters. Winifred Wigmore is the most vividly alive member of the first group because of the letters from Mary Ward, and through the personal knowledge she put into the biography she wrote with Mary Poyntz. At Augsburg there is a charming portrait of her, smiling, pen and paper in hand, ready to take down and preserve the wisdom of her friend.

Plate number 22 is the central picture in the Painted Life, shewing a handful of young women around their leader and teacher, embarking on lives of extraordinary danger, tumult, exhaustion and disappointment, each persevering to the end. All of them, except Mary Ward herself, died far from home.

The General Congregation of the Institute of the Blessed Virgin Mary, 1993

Sister M. Pia Buxton, Provincial Superior

The purpose of this account is to describe the General Congregation, which took place from July 30th to September 1st 1993, and thereby to help the readers of this book to put St Mary's Ascot into the much bigger context of the world-wide Institute which has communities, schools, tasks and challenges in every continent.

A General Congregation of the IBVM has not been held in England before. Such a gathering is made up of the Provincials and one or two elected delegates from each of the twenty-one Provinces, in this case making seventy-eight members in all, from about twenty countries. It is required to meet every nine years to elect a new General Superior and Council, or to re-elect the existing Sisters for a further six years. The outgoing Superior General gives an account of her nine years in office, and each Province reports on its life and activities. When reports and elections are completed delegates reflect upon, discuss and eventually vote upon proposals and recommendations for the coming years that are sent in from all over the world. A Congregation brings people up to date and renews their sense of belonging to a world-wide Institute; it brings a fresh vision of Mary Ward's purposes, and requires examination of how it can be fostered in each succeeding age and in every place. Without this continuous acquaintanceship with the changes in the world, a religious Institute would not make the necessary adaptations and would become extinct.

Today, there are about two thousand five hundred Sisters in the

Roman Branch of the Institute, divided into twenty-one Provinces. In some places numbers are diminishing and in some increasing. In Germany there are six Provinces with about one thousand Sisters in all. In Austria there is a Province of about seventy Sisters, in Italy two Provinces with a hundred and forty-five Sisters, in Spain about forty Sisters and in England about ninety. These are the old historical Provinces, all with shrinking numbers and top-heavy age structures. On the other hand new foundations have been made all over the world (especially from Germany); there are now two growing Provinces in India with about three hundred and thirty-five Sisters, one in Chile with seventy, one in Brazil with eighty-six, one in Argentina with thirty-five. In South Korea, where the first Foundation took place in 1964, there are nearly two hundred Sisters, all aged sixty or under. In the 1940s the Province of Mainz sent Sisters to Zimbabwe as it now is, to be followed later by Sisters from England, and the number of African Sisters is increasing noticeably. The collapse of the communist world has made it possible for four Provinces to come out after forty years of suppression, and to begin to breathe a new life: in Slovakia a hundred and sixty Sisters, in Hungary a hundred and twenty-two, in Rumania a hundred and twenty, and in the Czech Republic thirty. Very recently new foundations have been made in Siberia, the Ukraine and what was Eastern Germany.

At this Congregation of 1993 each of the other two branches of Mary Ward's Institute were represented for the first time—from the Generalates of the Irish Branch founded from York in 1820, and the North American Branch founded in Toronto from Dublin in 1848.

The text "Gather the people to me, that I may let them hear my words", which had prepared us all for the General Congregation, was fulfilled when we gathered in the Ascot chapel for the opening Mass. The brilliant and daring voices of the Campion Singers inspired hope and confidence in the delegates, the translators, facilitators, secretaries and visitors. It was a great occasion; everyone was a little amazed that it was happening and to find that everyone had arrived. The sound of the *Veni Sancte Spiritus* filled the chapel.

For the purposes of the work to be done, the gymnasium was transformed into an impressive Congregation Hall with booths for the translators at one end who, with the assistance of an attendant engineer, provided a very efficient instantaneous translation service.

The chief purpose of the Congregation, to elect a new General Superior, was fulfilled by the election of Sister Annuntiata Pak, along with a new Council. For the first time a non-European Sister of the Institute was chosen, who became the first Korean Sister to be elected as head of any international Order. These events took place in the second week of the Congregation, preceded by an account of the past nine years from the outgoing General, and by reports from the twenty-one Provincials. In Western Europe the story might have seemed depressing at first: the increasing burden of caring for elderly Sisters, the anxiety caused by the shortage of able-bodied Sisters to meet many major challenges. It would be easy in such circumstances to think it wise to retrench and regroup, to concentrate all energy on survival and the defence of what is already established. We needed to remind and refresh ourselves by remembering the manifold difficulties in the early history of the Institute, when Mary Ward never hesitated to make new Foundations in a spirit of prophetic faith and at times almost insane hope. The news that the Augsburg Province had made a new Foundation in Stuttgart, the Mainz Province one in Eastern Germany, and that the house at Passau had given one of its few active young Sisters to work in a much needed women's refuge brought a feeling of hope, and of new life growing out of death. The declining number of priests, even in traditional Catholic countries, has also brought change and opportunity to the IBVM. In Europe but also in Asia and Latin America, small groups of Sisters have taken over the pastoral care of parishes.

Mary Ward envisaged that her Sisters, like the early Jesuits before them, might go "among the Turks . . . or even to those who live in the region called the Indies". Today it is not towards the Indies but towards the seemingly unpromising lands of Siberia and China that the Institute turns its eyes, and work has already begun in Siberia in conditions of poverty and deprivation so familiar to our founders. In Eastern Europe—for whose Sisters we have prayed so long—we have to try to help them; their days of danger and suppression may be over, but they face the monumental task of trying to revive Catholic life and education in countries untouched by the spirit of Vatican II and where many aspects of the West are a source of bewilderment and dismay. The years of deprivation have left people vulnerable to the onslaught of the consumer culture; governments even now may be hostile, and the Institute's historic buildings have to be rescued from confiscation or ruin. But there is another way of looking at things: in Rumania alone there are now thirty novices, whereas all that the combined Western European Provinces can produce is nine novices between them.

In Latin America and India, the major challenge is the desperate poverty of the people. In both these continents relations with governments have not always been easy, but the fall of dictatorial regimes in Chile and Argentina has made it possible to develop a more comprehensive programme of evangelisation and staff training. There is good news of the spread of work amongst the very poorest parts of society in India and for example in Nepal; girls from IBVM schools in Europe are helping in this work.

South Korea was very much in people's minds after the election of Sister Annuntiata Pak. The respect for education there is legendary but there are many tensions, cultural and religious. The calls on the young Sisters are many, and at times eat into their need to complete their training; one recalls the frustration expressed by Mary Ward in her letters, when she was continuously badgered to send Sisters into ministeries before they had had time to prepare for them.

In Zimbabwe the rate of growth is slower, and the wounds after the years of civil war only just healing. As in other developing countries, the lack of educational opportunities for girls raises serious problems in the formation of those who feel called to the Institute. The spectre of Aids makes the situation of those to whom the Sisters minister increasingly desperate, but young women generously continue to come forward and the Kingdom of God grows from the tiniest of seeds.

During the final two weeks the Congregation was skilfully steered through the numerous and varied suggestions and proposals that had been sent in from all the Provinces. It is through reflection and discussion that the Institute may be led forward by the Spirit into renewal of mind and heart and to continuous scrutiny of its organisation. The Institute is not a monastic order and its members take no vow of stability in any sense. The ability to adapt and to change in response to need is one of its characteristics, and a restlessness of spirit, a physical and psychological freedom to move, are essential to its mission.

The General Congregation of 1993 shewed the opportunity as well as the urgent need to live fully the apostolic vocation as women, to fulfil the Constitutions inherited through Mary Ward from St Ignatius by bringing to them women's gifts and experiences: to be contemplative in action, to find God in all things.

We made three pilgrimages during the General Congregation, back into the roots of the Institute, to the story of Mary Ward and of the founding years and the places in which she and her followers lived—to St Omer, to Mary Ward's London and Mass in the crypt at Ely Place, and then on to the Bar Convent in York, to spend three days in the places that Mary Ward knew as a child, or to which she came back in 1640 for the last five years of her life. We visited the shrine of Our Lady at Mount Grace; Mulwith near Ripon where she was born; the valley of the River Nidd; Ripley Castle; Osgodby and eventually to the final closing Mass in the little Anglican Church at Osbaldwick in whose churchyard she was secretly buried, and where her massive gravestone makes its lasting impact on all who have come to know and love her. The Sisters gathered near her gravestone to celebrate the Eucharist and to pray before returning home on the following day. Such was the effect on those who were seeing this for the first time that they could scarcely be made to leave the church at the end. The huge, rough-hewn stone bears the inscription:

TO LOVE THE POORE
PERSEVER IN THE SAME
LIVE DY AND RISE WITH
THEM WAS ALL THE AYME
OF
MARY WARD WHO
HAVING LIVED 60 YEARES
AND 8 DAYES DYED THE
30 OF JAN. 1645.

The Congregation pondered these words. What do they mean for the Institute in the 1990s? There is no one, convenient answer for all places, but this is the challenge to be faced by the Institute as it looks towards the Twenty-First century—to find a way of loving the poor and persevering in this love while being faithful to its historic commitments in a changing world. If, in some senses, it is felt that the Institute is dying, then it is most surely rising as well, perhaps in poverty compared to the success and securities of the past, but also in faith and hope.

Education in the Bar Convent School in York in the Eighteenth Century

Sister M. Gregory Kirkus IBVM

"We must have a school for our daughters." These words are the Charter of the Bar Convent and of its school. They were spoken in 1686 by that grand old man, Thomas Gascoigne of Barnbow Hall and were addressed to Mother Frances Bedingfield of the Institute of Mary. They made a fine pair. Sir Thomas had been tried for his life on a charge of treason at the time of the supposed Titus Oates plot (1678), and although over eighty years of age he had narrowly escaped condemnation. Frances Bedingfield had already been twice in prison for her faith. They were a match for the establishment.

The words must have been music in Frances' ears, for the members of the Institute were suffering an "all-time low" in their fortunes. Their Foundress was dead, their Institute suppressed by Papal Bull with a great show of eloquence, they had no home of their own, and no work recognised by the Church to do. Sir Thomas matched his words with a gift of four hundred and fifty pounds and the promise of a yearly pension (which never materialised) and Frances Bedingfield, under the alias of Frances Long, purchased a house and garden. Undaunted by the laws forbidding the running of Catholic schools, the Sisters at once set up a school and invited the Catholic gentry to send their daughters to be educated "without Micklegate Bar".

By the beginning of the eighteenth century a community and school were established, as firmly as the laws of the time allowed. With the exception of a small house run by the Institute in

Hammersmith, it was the only school of its kind in England, and remained so for more than a hundred years.

The Superior in 1700 was Mother Dorothy Paston, as she called herself, really Paston-Bedingfield, a second cousin of Mother Frances. She had not the charisma of her cousin but she seems to have been a good Religious and an efficient business woman, as we see from the account books where each month's accounts are balanced and signed by her, and certain commitments are written off with a flourish—as "all paid long agoe" or "quite done with". (The finances of the house fell into sad disarray under her successor.) Members of the early community included Cicely Cornwallis (a very learned lady, as we shall see later on), Anna Magdalen Hugalin, Anne Mason, Helen Walker and Catharine Stanfield—ten in all. When admission of new members is set against the deaths of old ones, it would seem that the community did not rise above twelve, and was often below that figure until the last quarter of the century, when a modest rise to fourteen occurred. This little group of women not only taught the pupils, but cooked, washed and generally cared for them. Anne Mason was affectionately known as "Nanny" which suggests a happy relationship.

It was a secret community, concealing its identity under the general title of "the Ladies of the Bar". Its members wore slate-coloured gowns and hoods; they were addressed as "Mistress" rather than as Sister or Mother, and they were buried in nameless graves when they died. When Drake published the first edition of his *History and Antiquities of York* in 1736, by which time the Sisters had been there for fifty years, he says ambiguously that the house was often called the Nunnery but was really only a school for the daughters of Catholic families.

The lists of children of 1710 are lost but it is recorded that, in that year, there were some forty pupils. The number fell to about twenty between 1720 and 1735 before increasing steadily but not dramatically for the rest of the century. A Day School, sometimes unattractively called the Poor School, had also been founded by Mother Frances Bedingfield in 1699. It was a separate establishment, and no list of its pupils has survived, but as an equal number of day and boarding pupils was confirmed in 1773, the two schools may have been roughly comparable in numbers. A list of children admitted to the boarding school has been printed; it runs from 1710 to 1886 and is complete except for thirty-nine names that were on a missing leaf dealing with the years 1749 to 1753. A scrutiny of this register tells us much. In fulfilment of its purpose to educate the daughters of the Catholic gentry, it accepted Towneleys and Tempests, Stapletones and Scropes, Vavasours, Lawsons, Talberts, Cholmeys, Stourtons and so on. In the decade 1710 to 1720, ninety-one per cent of the intake was from northern homes; by the 1780s this proportion had declined to sixty-four per cent, indicating a widening catchment area, as the school's reputation became established. Though it was "upper class" it was never so much so as many of the Continental schools, for example, as that run by the Blue Nuns in Paris. Even in its early days it contained elements of the "middle class". In 1711, to give examples, Grace and Mary Palmes of Naburn, whose family kept a hat shop in York, were received as boarders and in 1735 Catherine Broomhead, the daughter of an iron manufacturer of Sheffield, was the first of four members of the family to be admitted.

As the century wore on and the Catholic gentry declined in numbers and became increasingly impoverished through recusancy fines, the "middle class" element became more pronounced. The Humbles of Newcastle, coal dealers and colliery managers, sent their daughters in 1760 and 1771 and they were joined by two Warburton girls from the same town. From Sheffield came a whole tribe of Eyres, and also the Smelter girls, whose occupational surname suggests the origin of the family fortunes. More surprising, perhaps, is the entry of Margaret and Eliza Langdale whose family were gin distillers in London. Merchants' daughters abounded in the later years of the century. It may be reasonably assumed that Mary Waths from Madeira, Anne and Bridget Farrell and Mary Brown from the West Indies, Catherine Daly from India and Mary Brownbill and Mary Jump of Liverpool all came from merchant families. The questions in mind must be, "How did these disparate elements mix, in so class-conscious an age? What did the Hon. Mary Fairfax of Gilling Castle and the Hon. Mary Vavasour of Hazlewood Castle make of their contemporary Mary Barrow of Newcastle? And a little later, how did the Hon. Mary Stourton of Stourton Park react to Harriet Fox of Sheffield?" We do not know, of course, but there is a clue in an entry in the journal. It runs, "October 20th 1772, Mr Humble came to fetch his daughter who against her will leaves us, but is resolved to come again to us if possible." So the atmosphere was not such as to alienate a collier's daughter.

But rich or poor, aristocratic or middle class, the pupils all shared the same life-style and there seems to have been little luxury, or even of what we should consider comfort. Mother Davies was Procuratrix (or, in modern terminology, housekeeper) from 1735 to 1741 and she kept a detailed account, in a black exercise book, of all that was bought, mended or adapted during those years. Her successors continued the journal up to 1772 (under the misnomer "Anecdotes of the Bar") and from these pages we can construct a very vivid picture of the economics of the Convent. The community seems to have lived on, if not below, the poverty line. Their chairs and beds were re-bottomed with old sacks, and their bed coverlets were made of discarded gowns, and old rags, their furniture fashioned from old cheese boards and workboxes. The "misses" as the children were called, rightly fared better. They had new ticks for their beds, new pegs to hang their clothes on and their pillows were filled with feathers fresh from Lincolnshire. A tea-pot and tea-cups with handles were purchased for them, even though tea was scarce and expensive. Nevertheless life was very spartan, for we learn from the account books that tea and sugar had to be paid for. Washing facilities consisted of two "commodious" basins placed near one of the school-rooms, and the more energetic children raced down, eager for the "first dip and a dry towel". There were said to be occasional baths in Fulford, but I can find no trace of information about these visits.

A study of contemporary prints of the little old house, leads me to the conclusion that living conditions during the first half of the century must have been dreadfully crowded and no doubt the "misses" viewed with excitement the demolition of the house and the execution of extensive new building plans. Mother Ann Aspinall, herself an old pupil of the school, was the inspirator of the whole project. She had vision, good taste and business acumen, and under her guidance the school had grown in numbers. But in the 1760s, the community was still poor and Mother Aspinall had to do some fund-raising for her ambitious designs. From a contemporary "list of those who were so generous as to help with the building of our new house" we learn that she received contributions from the nobility and gentry (Lord Petre, Lady Arundell, Lady Gerard etc.) and also from the tradespeople of York, who evidently felt some kinship with the community. First came the foundation of the new chapel, without leave or licence of course. "It is said", wrote Mother Aspinall proudly to the Chief Superior of Munich, "that when completed it will be the handsomest and most commodious in these parts", and the children must have shared the nuns' pride when it was used for the first time on April 27th 1769. Gradually the living accommodation spread round the open courtyard (Drake speaks in his second edition of "elegant building backwards") and finally the space was enclosed when "Ann Aspinall, Spinster, of the suburbs of York" received a licence to build a "new front wall to her house". Hence the present-day facade; but it was 1790 before the clock-face was put into the pediment, and by then Ann Aspinall was dead, and so was Henry Hindley who had built the turret clock that marked the timetable of nuns and children alike.

When we consider the school day, it has to be admitted that we know very little of the eighteenth-century curriculum, but there is no doubt that the nuns were well-educated women, and took the education of the children very seriously. Cecily Cornwallis, we are told, was learned in Hebrew, Greek, astronomy, philosophy and mathematics, as well as Latin and other European languages. Mother Horbery had been in Munich, and Mother Mary Partington, says a contemporary letter, "speaks Latin, French and Italian like her mother tongue". The fluency of the nuns in languages and the evidence of the books in the "antique library" and of the early correspondence (much carried on in elegant French) suggests a curriculum in which languages predominated long before it was fashionable for French to be taught in all upper-class schools. This theory is corroborated by the rules for the Prefect of Studies, who is enjoined "to take great notice that the Convictors (i.e. boarders) who are sent to us in order to learn languages, exercise themselves in speaking them, not permitting that they speak any other tongye, it being evident that this is the easiest and the readiest way to understand any language". In addition, there were to be translation exercises, and passages were to be learnt by heart.

The library (an unusual feature for a group of women to own in the eighteenth century) must have played an important part in the formation of the children's minds. It was no exercise in appearances, for the books are well worn and some are annotated with marginal notes. Although the majority are on religious subjects, there are also histories and a surprising number of books on travel—on Japan, "New France" or Canada, and on Paraguay. We do not know how large the library was, but some fifteen hundred old volumes have survived.

In addition to the more academic subjects, we know that italic handwriting was taught and that "musick" could sometimes include the guitar, as one pupil had to pay for the hire of such an instrument. Drawing and painting were the accomplishments that all young ladies must learn, and we have Mr Joseph Halfpenny's bill for the time spent on instruction and for the materials supplied. Needlework included embroidery and, it would seem, dressmaking. Dancing was a popular extra in the eighteenth century, before it became rather frowned upon in the narrower, stricter atmosphere of the succeeding century.

Although details of the academic life of the school are nebulous, enough is known to prove that great value was set upon education. In November 1772, Mother Aspinall wrote, "Our school flourishes, and I have often great praises of the young ladies who have left us, from their parents and friends. This is a great satisfaction and a great encouragement to those who took so much pains with their education." A generation later, Mother Coyney (herself a Bar Pupil) "made no secret of her preference for those who possessed minds", and she "used to say that she could not endure to see women with children's heads on their shoulders." Perhaps this sounds a little intellectually snobbish, and to redress the balance we should study the Rules for the Prefects of Schools and for "those who teach in our schools." Here it is made clear that the "chief end" of their office is to care for their pupils' souls, and that example is much more important than precept. The teacher must have a humble bearing, must "avoid hastiness of speech, with sharp and biting words, correcting and admonishing in a spirit of mildness those she has charge of", and again, "she must not shew more love or inclination to one more than another . . . but shew a general propension and affection towards all."

Having in mind how small and precarious the community was, one must admire the integrity of Rule 22, which reads: "If any she has the care of should entertain thought embracing a Religious state, and is not inclined to one Order more than another, she must not encline her in any way and least of all towards our Institute, but leave her to be resolved of her indifferancy by Almighty God who gave her that vocation." This rule must have been faithfully kept for, of the thirty-three members professed during the eighteenth century, only sixteen had been educated in the Bar Convent, while more than as many again joined other Orders. Lastly, the golden rule of all pedagogy is expressed quaintly but succinctly in Rule 13. "She must observe the wit and capacity of every one in particular, and so accommodate her instructions to the measure of their understandings, that those who are advanced may advance farther and those who are more backward be not neglected." We today can do no better than that.

When we consider the daily life of the children, a much clearer picture emerges. Perhaps the most outstanding feature is that there were no school holidays, as we know them today, when trunks are packed and dormitories and classrooms are emptied for a breathing-space of some weeks. The girls came to school for a period of two of three years, sometimes longer, and normally spent the whole of the time in the Convent. But some qualifications must be made to this statement. First, I do not believe that families living in, say, Yorkshire, Lancashire or Durham, did not send for their daughters to attend such occasions as the wedding of an older brother or sister. Why else should there be items such as "coach hire" in the bills, midway through a child's school career? But these were exceptional events. Secondly, there were certainly holidays from lessons, and in Mother Davies' notebook we catch a glimpse of visits to St Luke's Fair in the Autumn and to another fair at Pentecost. The "misses" were given "spending money" with which to have some fun, while Mother Davies made more serious purchases of delph porringers and mugs. At Christmas there must have been a Nativity Play, as a bag for the Kings' hair is made, and new crooks are provided for the shepherds. Other recreational items are recorded in the notebook. Mother Davies bought a cribbage board, a Fox and Geese board, a book of Robberies and a copy of *Robinson Crusoe*. Even the latter must have been hailed as a thriller, especially as the book opens with the sentence "I was born in the city of York".

Out of doors, there were no sports or organised games, but the scene sounds pleasant enough. Drake speaks of the "site, the gardens and the agreeable walles beyond" being very suitable for a school, and the notebook gives us more details. It tells of "pathes new gravelled", grass plats or lawns, a brick "arber", with two new wooden seats set nearby. The "little garden" is turned into "a garden more profitable than asparagus was". The strawberry bed in the "great garden" is dug up and half of it planted with raspberries, and rosemary set against all the buttresses in the garden wall. For animal lovers, there was the "young whelp" and the "dogg" and if the "misses" were allowed to stray into the farm area there was a pig and a hog, sheep and even a cow to interest them. For the younger children, kind Mother Davies provided "a swing for the Misses to ride in". The notebook exudes a humane atmosphere and the children were probably happy, especially as the majority had sisters or cousins in the school to give them family support.

We have not yet exhausted the archival material with which to bring to life the eighteenth-century school. As we move into the second half of the century, the children's bills, complete from 1761 onwards, are a rich source of information. I have pored over them until I could almost hear the scratching of the quill pens that write them, and the sigh of relief as the accountant inscribed "all paid". Since the pupils lived permanently at school, the nuns had to provide for all their needs, and chief among these were their clothes which had to be purchased and repaired. "New stays" and "stays amending" and "letting out" suggest healthy growing girls, and shoes also had often to be "amended". There is mention of cambric for tuckers, cotton stockings, mits and gloves. A quilted petticoat must have been a very welcome addition to one's wardrobe, when "a fire in the bedchamber" was an extra, while a "calamanco petticoat" must have combined warmth and beauty; calamanco was a satin-twilled woollen stuff, checkered or brocaded in the warp.

Other items dispel all fears that the Convent was a kill-joy institution. There is gold and silk for watch-strings, ruffles, a straw hat and a silk hat; and what a wonderful dress Amelia Farquharson must have made for herself in 1769 out of eleven and a half yards of pink, green and white lustring. (Lustring or lutestring was a glossy silk material.) Spending money occurs quite often, and so do Valentines in February. In 1764 Mary Swinburne must have had some cause for a great celebration, as "spending money amongst companions, 4s" is itemised, while on the next lines "wine, chickens, bisketts, rolls and a Valentine" are all put together with a suggestion of festivity. "Hire of a chair" occurs fairly frequently in the bills and must refer to a Sedan chair, perhaps to transport one of the misses to the Assembly Rooms for a concert, or even a ball. "Portage of letters" was the equivalent of postage stamps, for correspondence with home. More seriously "tooth, 2s 6d" suggests a nasty moment for Mary Dalton, and, "bleeding leeches" are better not thought of.

We can add further details to our picture book of Convent life by examining a recipe book of 1753. It could hardly look more authentic; dog-eared and dirty, it obviously spent most of its working life on the kitchen table. It contains a number of recipes for cakes and wines (damson wine, lemon cake, ginger cake, Shrewsbury cakes, seed-cake and rich pan-cakes) that must all have cheered the 'misses' on feast-days. Cream cheese is made in a brick mould with rushes laid on the board, and an orange pudding sounds rather rich with its ingredients of 8oz of sugar, 5oz of butter and 5 eggs, but no flour! These recipes are artlessly mixed with remedies for rheumatism, King's Evil and various common maladies. There is a concoction for the voice that includes "an oz of garlic and a gill of best old rhum", an eye ointment and a bitter draught that sounds quite lethal with its compound of wormwood water and gentian seed.

Medical care was everywhere primitive, and death was no stranger to the Bar Convent; nor did it spare the children. Mother Aspinall writes, on April 21st 1767, "It has pleased our good God to send me a cross in the death of one of our pensioners (children) of consumption. I have felt it intensely. Her father, who loved her most tenderly received the news of his loss with true Christian resignation, and to testify his conviction and satisfaction that every possible care had been taken by us of his dear child, he made me a considerable present." Nearly a year later, another letter brings further bad news; "I trust that you have escaped the malady that has for some time reigned in these parts, especially amongst children, ulcerated sore throats accompanied with fever. With this the majority of our children have been attacked, and I have had the misfortune to lose one, a child of high rank. She was quite well when seized with the epidemic which carried her off in 40 hours." Then there is the poignant story of Mary Clifton, related only, as far as I can find, in a single page of the account book. She came to school in December 1765 and was at first a very normal child. She had lawn and cambric for her ruffles, pomatum and combs for her hair, and a scarlet cloak, but halfway down the page the items become a little sinister, with indications of special care such as "a fire in her bedchamber . . . tea, chocolate, sugar, wine and biskets". Worse follows with "to the doctor . . . to the surgeon . . . the apothcaries' bills . . . and wax candles . . . a fine crape burial suite . . . coffin, church fees, under bearers and a velvet pall".

Nearly all the nuns and children who died in the Convent during the eighteenth century are buried in Holy Trinity, Micklegate, either in the churchyard under nameless slabs still to be seen in the corner by Trinity Lane, or in the Chancel of the Church, where the exact spots are unidentifiable. I never go down Micklegate without thinking of "ours" who lie buried there and since the penal laws forbade the burial of Catholics in Anglican graveyards, I used to puzzle about what sort of funerals they had. Were the laws sufficiently relaxed to allow full Catholic rites, or were the burials carried out secretly at midnight? I had resigned myself never to know the answer, but recently I discovered a clue. An entry in a journal reads: "23rd September 1777, Mistress Jane Charge took to the Infirmary". She was an old sister and on October 8th "she died in her chair as if in a slumber". On the 11th a dirge was sung for her and she was "carried to her grave between 6 and 7 at night". So that was it—not a dramatic midnight event, but a discreet burial as dusk was deepening into darkness and all the inhabitants of Micklegate would be indoors by their firesides. And no doubt that sad cortege bearing the body of little Mary Clifton also wended its way in the dark; and after the burial the velvet pall was folded up, the wax candles extinguished, and the mourners returned through Micklegate Bar to the Convent for the wine and biscuits that are the last item on her bill.

To return to the living, let it not be thought that the children's world was circumscribed by the walls of the Convent or that their outlook was limited to the daily round of lessons, recreations, and trivialities. The events of the outside world impinged more upon the members of the community and the school than we might expect, and probably more than they did in the nineteenth century. We must remember that non-enclosure was an essential, and at that time unique, feature of the IBVM, so members of the community went out into the city visiting the sick and the poor, and their friends and relations came to the Convent for help, social visits and even for business advice and financial support. And there must have been a great deal of exchange of news and views, especially as the town houses of northern nobility and gentry lined the street of Micklegate. One entry in the journal reads: "Mr Bedingfield called with songs he had written, and stayed two hours". He seems to have outstayed his welcome on that occasion, but how much better then was the community's open attitude than that expressed later in a rule for the portress which enjoined "When the bell rings she shall go to the door and dismiss with as few words as possible those of the opposite sex".

The Convent was a gathering place for information about events of national importance, and the pupils must have been well aware of what was going on. Even though the Catholic families of the time played only a small part in the Jacobite Rebellions of 1715 and 1745, sympathy and old loyalties must have been aroused, the march of the Jacobite armies followed with keen interest. Henry Hindley was questioned when he came to see the clock. As the '45 army retreated from Derby up the north-western side of the Pennines, no "active service" would have been seen in York, but the nuns could not possibly have shielded the misses' tender eyes from the grisly sight of the severed heads of two Jacobites, James Mayne and William Connolly, exposed on Micklegate Bar. It has been conjectured that the page torn out of the admissions register of the school was destroyed because it included a name from an actively Jacobite family—an entry that might have been damaging to the Convent. Whatever the truth of that, the '45 Rebellion had a delayed action upon the Community—a repercussion that was nearly disastrous for the school.

There was in the city a Dr Jacques Sterne, uncle of the novelist Lawrence Sterne. His grandfather had been Archbishop of York, and he himself was a Canon Residentiary, Precentor and Prebendary of York, Prebendary of Durham and Rector of the parishes of Rise and Hornsey-cum-Riston in the East Riding of the county. This formidable man had received an accolade for his zealous support of the Hanoverians in the Rising of 1745 and he seems to have wanted to ingratiate himself further with the powers of the Establishment. The Convent appeared to be an easy target, so in 1748 he called on the nuns and told the Superior, Mother Hodshon, that she must dismiss the pupils and quit the house, with the whole community by the 22nd August. The nuns were clearly shaken, all the more when he threatened, if not obeyed, to bring the full weight of the penal laws upon them. There were plenty of penal laws that the nuns were transgressing, so it was a very serious situation. Their friend Lord Fairfax came to York, asked to see all the Community in the parlour and advised them to disperse—at least until the storm should blow over. They were about to give way, when Mother Eleonara Clifton settled the matter by saying "I have consecrated myself to the service of God to labour for the salvation of souls in the house, and, whilst a wall of it is standing, I will never leave it. If they drag me out I cannot help it, but I will never go otherwise." This robust resolution gave heart to the other Sisters and all decided to defy Dr Sterne. He was as good (or as bad) as his word and had the Superior and a companion cited to appear before the Spiritual Court. They were charged with not attending the Protestant parish church and not receiving the Sacrament on a certain day specified for all to receive it. However, the case was very ill-prepared, as the indolent vicar had not administered Holy Communion to anyone on that day. So the case was dismissed and the two Sisters returned home to be greeted by a much relieved community. I do not know whether the children knew what danger their school had been in; but I think they did, as a Te Deum was recited in thanksgiving, and public devotions to St Michael ordered for May 8th.

The French Revolution had a more tangible impact upon the inhabitants of the Convent. The girls must have heard the rumblings of the storm from the very beginning, as so many Catholic families had ties of friendship and kinship with the French aristocracy. The scene became more vivid with the arrival of refugees. As early as 1789 the father of Charlotte and Yolsei Bonneuil foresaw the danger, and brought his two daughters to England and placed them at school in the Convent to complete their education. Charlotte was a fashionable and rather worldly Parisienne of twenty, but she settled down to life in the Convent and eventually asked to be admitted to the novitiate in 1791. She lived a very saintly life for two years and died in 1793. Anne Sophie de Rocher left her home in Brittany in 1794, taught French and Drawing in the school and also died young in 1799. Louise de Guyon Beaufort's story is the most tragic of all. Her family owned large estates and her father was an avowed royalist, so he and his family were in immediate danger. He sent his wife and two daughters to York, but optimistically viewed this as a short-term precautionary measure. They brought no warm clothing with them, a lack that was made good from the misses' wardrobes. This same optimism led Louise's mother and sister to return to France, deluded by false assurances of security. Her whole family, including her brother, perished on the guillotine.

These individuals were not the only victims of the Revolution encountered by the Bar Convent. The stream of refugees included priests and nuns. The Superior at the time was Mother Catherine Rouby, a very compassionate woman who used to send out her "spies" as she called them to watch the coaches coming in to York. French men and women were assumed to be priests and nuns, and were directed to the Convent. Some six thousand priests came to England, and a fair proportion of these found their way to York. One of them, Fr Louis de Henne, became chaplain to the Community, and Mother Rouby found work for many others in the city where they taught French and Drawing. Perhaps the misses joined in the early morning sessions when the nuns sewed shirts for the more impoverished. They shewed their gratitude to Mother Rouby by gifts of books and by the three alabaster statues now at the back of the chapel.

Refugee nuns sometimes came in whole communities—the Carmelites from Brabant, who arrived in such dire straits that the York Sisters wept to see them, the Poor Clares from Rouen and the Canonesses of the Holy Sepulcre from Liège. The community gave up their beds, and I think the children must have joined in the sacrifice in order to provide hospitality for these exiles, before they moved on to more permanent homes.

Thus the nuns and the "misses" (soon to be known as the young ladies) reached the end of a century of struggle and achievement, and not least was the achievement of survival. In addition to the inestimable legacy of their Faith, they have left us unique annals, a gracious building and many beautiful artifacts by which we may remember them.

Mother M. Campion Davenport IBVM, 1878 to 1970

Mother Campion has been mentioned already in chapter six, when I remarked that she was one of the more outstanding teaching Sisters who did not become headmistress. There were others, and in Music particularly, Mother Ancilla and Mother Barbara; their organ-playing and singing is warmly remembered by Old Girls of many generations. Mother Campion nevertheless seems to have been of a rather different kind, not necessarily entirely attractive but certainly greatly gifted.

The present Director of Music at St Mary's, Gareth Lloyd, says that when he was appointed in September 1991, he was taken by Sister Cecily (who has since died) to look over a number of dusty boxes which contained the music of Mother Campion. This had been written, so she always maintained, only because liturgical music suitable for girls to sing in choir was so hard to come by. It had been more or less forgotten since her death. Now, her music has become a central part of the repertoire of a specialist chamber choir in the school of forty girls between the ages of eleven and eighteen. They have taken the name of The Campion Singers and have already performed in many churches and halls; they have made a CD recording of her music, and in July 1993 went on a successful concert tour in Canada.

She was born Muriel Winifred Davenport, from a well-known Cheshire family. Her father returned as a young man to the Catholic Faith of his ancestors, gave up his profession of barrister and went to the Royal Academy of Music where he became, in due course, Professor of Harmony and Counterpoint, and married the Principal's daughter.

Muriel Davenport shewed musical talent at a very early age, playing the piano, especially the music of Bach, when she was five and singing in oratorios. She said that she was aware of a religious vocation at the age of four, but her mother was adamantly against any such thing. At eighteen, she left home to live in London, to have piano lessons with Eugénie Schumann, daughter of Robert and Clara. In 1890, she went to study at the Dresden Conservatoire. From there she followed a concert career, either as solo pianist, or with her great friend, the Swedish singer, Maja Kjôhler; they were known as "the Nightingale and the Star". She became a great friend of Gustav Holst's, and apparently it was she who suggested the name Imogen for his daughter. During the First World War, she worked as a nurse in Salonika, and was invalided out seriously ill.

Almost all this information comes from papers written by Sister Margaret Mary Littlehales IBVM. She did not mention that Muriel Davenport taught music at Bedales for five years, from 1910 to 1915. I discovered this myself entirely by accident, looking through the Bedales Roll of former staff and pupils, though different editions give different dates; I am taking those that seem most reasonable. I can find no means of knowing about her life there, because there is no-one alive who remembers her. There is no doubt that she would have come under the influence of Oswald Powell, the second master and in a sense co-founder of Bedales with John Haden Badley. Powell's significance is that he had been a pupil at Uppingham when Dr Thring was headmaster, and remained closely in touch with the school always. Thring had transformed an unimportant country grammar school into a major public school, and was the convenor of the first meeting of the Headmasters' Conference. He made music, instrumentally and chorally, a central part of the life of his school, so that no boy could escape its reaches. Uppingham was the first school to take music so seriously, and Powell, his disciple, took this on to Bedales. Muriel Davenport joined a highly gifted music staff; every day ended with a musical performance by pupils and staff or pupils only, and there was great emphasis on choral music, whether in small or large groups or with the whole school.

I do not know what happened to her between leaving Bedales to nurse in Salonika and 1924, except that she resumed her musical career. In that year, at the age of forty-five, she entered the Institute, taking the name of Campion because she felt some affinity with the career of St Edmund Campion. I do not know why she chose the IBVM and I do not know what affinity she felt with Edmund Campion. She was at Ascot for the next twenty-three years, in charge of the music where she achieved astonishingly high standards. "I only wrote things because they were needed, and having fulfilled that requirement, said 'enough'." She remained an outstanding pianist; on the occasion when she gave a recital in the Wigmore Hall in November 1923, the *Morning Post* had written: "Would that all pianists who come before the public were on such good terms with their art as is Miss Muriel Davenport." Her playing of Beethoven was praised particularly, but she had a vast repertoire, to which (I believe it because I am told) she added the Liszt B Minor Sonata when she was nearly eighty. Many remember her as a great teacher, though the school magazine indicates lacunae. Antonia Fraser, looking back to a much later year—1946—remembers quite fruitless piano lessons with her.

Her life at Ascot stopped when she was sent to Rome in 1947, to become General Assistant to the Mother General and Superior to the Rome House. She was a great linguist and became perfect in Italian. Apparently she loved especially the sonnets of Michelangelo, "My darling who never took his stockings off". (This is a reference to the story in Vasari's *Lives of the Artists* that as an old man Michelangelo took to wearing boots made out of dog skin, which he did not take off for months at a time. When he did *his* skin tended to come away with them.) She was equally attracted to David: "both were sinners, but both so blessedly alive". To tell the truth, this bewilders me.

She lived in Rome and in Castel Gandolfo, and played a considerable part in bringing together the three Generalates of the IBVM. During these years, she was much in correspondence with Mother Cecilia Marshall. Her letters to Mother Cecilia are not to be found, but I have drawn on a selection made by Sister Mark of Mother Cecilia's letters to Mother Campion. Obviously they held each other in great esteem. I am told that Mother Cecilia valued her views and advice above those of all others. On her return from Rome, Mother Campion was Superior in Cambridge from 1955 to 1961, and played a considerable part in the life of the school there. She returned to Ascot at the age of eighty-three and immersed herself in translating writings concerning Mary Ward. She continued to read widely in many languages, studied Teilhard de Chardin ("miles beyond me but I still love the man"), and in the year before she died began to read Goethe. She lived so long that she outlived her friends. Maja Kjôhler died five months before her.

Mother Campion died in October 1970. There are Sisters and others who remember her. She was a powerful woman, and much of what I have been told about her—particularly her attitude to younger Sisters, and her habit of correcting what she saw as other people's faults, whether in knowledge, pronunciation or punctuation—does not make her seem likeable. Certainly she was not a conventional nun, but an exacting, acerbic teacher, with not overmuch patience. In her time, the sight of her playing the piano with a cigarette at one corner of her mouth must have seemed outlandish. Her language could be strong and colourful and her opinions were never mild. When one hears her music, it seems out of character. It was written with liturgical occasions and adolescent girls in mind. It is technically accomplished, but stylistically sub-Fauré, even sentimental. Gareth Lloyd tells me that right at the end of her life she set some poems by Goethe that are completely different in style and quality, but I have not heard them.

Reflections by the Bursar, 1985 to 1993

Group Captain Philip Callan.

I came to St Mary's in the Summer of 1985 a year after the transition to lay management had been introduced. It was apparent from the outset that the key to success depended upon a harmonious handover of responsibility from the IBVM to the Governing Body. It was fortunate that the Headmistress, Sister Mark Orchard, and the Chairman of Governors, Mr Julian Bell, were clearheaded about their respective roles and able to give much needed help and guidance about the way forward. This was especially necessary in my own case as I had little idea how a boarding school worked; much later I came to recognise that a medium-size boarding school is probably the most difficult type to manage economically as similar facilities are required to those in a school twice the size. Some management structures had been put in place: the accounts office and an administrative office had been set up with the aid of a generous donation from a benefactor. There was no overall co-ordination of the various functions apart from that provided by the Headmistress, already burdened with educational matters. Many other organisational matters required urgent attention.

My first day in office gave me a very good idea of how others saw my role. I opened my new office door to be confronted by a bicycle parked upside down with a wheel missing, apparently awaiting my instant attention. There were notes of known and potential problems, for example blocked drains, dangerous wires, and shortcomings in many areas. I was soon to be visited by the then head of a contracting company who promised to "scratch my back if I scratched hers". On my second day I went to the accounts office to find we were carrying an overdraft. It was only a small overdraft and it was close to the end of the financial year, but it was a disconcerting discovery. I promised myself there and then that we would never again have such a situation and that as far as possible we would not have a loan.

There was a lot to be done to fulfil the aims of the newly appointed Governing Body. However, Julian Bell was a very experienced school governor and he provided the framework for the way forward. A long-term strategy meeting was held to set out the aims of the School over the next ten years. It is remarkable to look back at the list of items that came from that meeting and to realise that virtually every one of the original objectives has now been achieved. In particular, the £3 million building programme provided for the new Science Block, Swimming Pool, staff housing, and the up-grading of essential facilities.

Several major defects in the school's financial structure had to be addressed. Firstly, the fees were inadequate for the changed circumstances. The IBVM had been generous in previous years and there was an understandable reluctance to raise fees beyond the minimum required. However, the need to provide lay teachers to replace the diminishing number of IBVM teachers dictated change. Large fee increases followed, fuelled by increasingly high rates of inflation. In September 1984 the fees were set at £4,120 a year and ten years later in September 1993 they were set at £10,995. The largest rise was 21.6% in 1990, following a 17.8% rise in 1989, and the smallest was the rise of 4.5% in 1993. After ten years of significant fee increases St Mary's is now equal to other girls' boarding schools in the area. Parents will be relieved to know that there is no race to compete with boys' schools of similar standing in terms of fees.

Bursaries were reviewed and a new means-tested system introduced to ensure the fair allocation of limited funds. A new charitable trust was formed to separate the bursary finances from those of the main school, and it was planned in the longer term to create a fund to support some scholarships. The Old Girls' Association decided to put their bursary money into the school's charitable trust, so enhancing income and saving on bank charges. The charitable trust is managed by a group drawn from the main School Trust, the Old Girls' Association, the IBVM, and two independent advisors. Bursaries are awarded on the recommendation of a sub-committee chaired by a school governor who must remain anonymous.

In the early stages the audits of accounts were carried out by a large London partnership which also audited the IBVM Provincialate funds. In that the school was in a particular relationship to the Provincialate as a tenant of 44 acres of the 55-acre IBVM Ascot estate, there was reasonable anxiety about a possible conflict of interest if both parties employed the same auditor. The school therefore appointed its own, a small local firm for which the school's accounts were a major element in its business, and its fees more in line with the school's expenditure. It was decided to give separate budgets to all heads of department, so ensuring that each budget holder was aware of expenditure limits and helped by monthly reports and, therefore, better able to plan the management of their resources. This system also had the "spin-off benefit" of introducing educationally-minded people to the discipline of accountability [I love this phrase: author].

The school budget is administered under a number of headings. Income headings are: Fees Receivable, Letting Fees and Miscellaneous Receipts. Expenditure Headings are: Establishment, Administration, Educational, Departmental and Financial. There are sixty-four separate budgets within these general headings to differentiate between the various activities and to enable a sensible distribution of responsibility to heads of department. The largest expense is salaries, taking 57.6% of expenditure. The upkeep of buildings and estate takes a further 12%.

The provision of a computer-based accounts system was part of the 1984 plan. This gave a much-needed sophisticated means for management with the potential for development. When the time came to replace the first system in 1989/90 there was considerable debate about whether or not an integrated school management system should be introduced. There were those who urged caution lest non-accountants and particularly teachers should get into the system and ruin everything. It was decided to instal an integrated network to link the school's primary database with the accounting package; rapid dissemination was ensured, and everyone using the system knew that they were referring to the most up-to-date information. Features included word processing facilities, a spreadsheet package and an appeal control system.

As parents well know, schools use Appeals to keep fees down. St Mary's has had two very successful Appeals in the last ten years. The idea behind the 1986/87 Appeal is interesting; the School officially was seeking to provide a new Science Block, but behind this there was an unspoken desire by many parents and governors to replace the old outdoor swimming pool by a new indoor heated pool. The Appeal managed to do both. The 1992 Appeal was remarkably fruitful in a period of recession and, to everyone's amazement, enabled the Upper Sixth Form Courtyard to be created. These two Appeals were successful because they were directed with great professionalism by Bernard Ashford, helped by Sister Mark, Sister Bridget as President of the AOGA, and the two Chairwomen of Appeals, the Hon Mrs Olga Polizzi (1986/87), and Lady Cecil Cameron (1992).

To turn now to the administrative staff structure, which has been developed to be the most cost effective in its use of people and resources. There are several key elements in the life of a boarding school and for its pupils; next to getting a day off study or perhaps more importantly a letter from home or, even better, a letter from a boy friend, comes food. The catering arrangements, once the IBVM Sisters who had provided these had left, became unsatisfactory. A contract caterer lasted only four months. Then came a "cordon bleu trained" supervisor of an untrained group of housewives who not only catered but took on cleaning and laundry duties. In the event, we finally decided to have our own staff and were fortunate to obtain the services of an outstanding catering manager/chef, Ron

Curran, who brought in a wide experience of institutional catering. The variety of food provided was vastly improved and the cost per pupil per day reduced. To have in-house staff is remarkably comforting.

The pressure of work coming from a multitude of new demands required the appointment of a Works Manager. All through these years, Sister Isabelle continued as Domestic Bursar, and managed this in addition to the great responsibility of being Head of Babthorpe until September 1991; these duties never prevented her from her wonderful creative work behind the scenes for drama and other costumed events. A new lay housekeeper has now replaced Sister Isabelle who remains as sacristan of the Chapel and continues to support the drama department. She continues also to display her great skill in producing dried flowers for Bazaar Days. Sister Hilary performs many useful and unsung roles and Sister Gabriel continues to be active in the laundry when not secretly taking additional supplies of food to keep the works staff happy.

Security is a particularly sensitive area; too much makes for a prison and none at all is too great a risk. We have settled for the time being on a system of site patrols each evening and for random visits by the guards to check selected areas during the night. Soon we shall have an in-house caretaker.

Relationships with teaching staff, parents and children represent different challenges. Teachers are very sensitive and must be handled with care. They know the bursar is out to restrict their pay, ask them to justify their many demands for more resources, make a fuss because they have parked on the grass, and complain when they use the photocopier to run off x copies of *The Times* Crossword. Parents are different, almost as important as teachers; in fact they are most important to a bursar because they finance the school budget. Fortunately, the majority of them is quite resigned to paying about £80,000 to have each daughter educated so long as the school lives up to its reputation for producing well-balanced and well-qualified young ladies at the end of their Sixth Form career. All parents must be treated with respect and courtesy whilst taking account of their human foibles. Some develop forgetfulness or calculated naiveté when it comes to dealing with the dreaded fee invoice. These characteristics are to be found mostly in fathers whilst mothers cast eagle eyes over the charges for extras, and so initiate a regular exchange of letters at the beginning of term. The bursar has few contacts with pupils apart from giving the occasional talk about money or berating them for some minor infringement. Occasionally there are petitions such as the ones I received in 1987 about the Gilmuire House showers signed by Belinda, Camille, Melanie, Emma, Henri, Caroline, Natasha and Lara. One or two came in verse and so I was able finally to respond thus:

The Saga of the Gilmuire Shower

Dear little girls of the House of Gilmuire,
I know you all want to be clean and pure.
Alas the contractor has gone off the site
And so you are dirty all through the night.

Your pleas have jolted the bursar awake;
His words to the contractor have made the man quake.
So hopefully soon you will have a nice shower
And once again smell as fresh as a flower.

The Sixth Form Ball is the time when the bursar sees most of the girls in every sense. We started these in the Art Department, then moved to Ascot Race Course where we had security problems, then to the Building Confederation Headquarters where the problems persisted, finally finishing up with our own marquee Ball to which parents are invited.

All in all, the life of a bursar is what he makes it. It would be easy to be overwhelmed by the volume and range of the work. Patience and constant alertness are the order of the day. The most important aspect in keeping one's sanity is in ensuring a harmonious working relationship with the Chairman of Governors and Headmistress, and at the same time fostering the closest communications with the IBVM Province who, after all, created the school, inspired it and gave it the means to help it flourish.

Provincials of the Institute of the Blessed Virgin Mary from 1929, Superiors and Headmistresses since 1885

PROVINCIALS

1. Reverend Mother Cecilia Marshall, 1929–60
2. Reverend Mother Perpetua Lawler, 1960–72
3. Reverend Mother Gregory Kirkus, 1972–82
4. Reverend Mother Francis North, 1982–90
5. Reverend Mother Pia Buxton, 1991–

SUPERIORS

1. Mother Joseph Edwards, 1885–1901
2. Mother Teresa Blagden, 1901–13
3. Mother Cecilia Marshall, 1913–59
4. Mother Perpetua Lawler, 1959–67
5. Mother Magdalen Ingram, 1967–70
6. Sister Isabelle McIrvine, 1970–9
7. Sister Agatha Leach, 1979–82
8. Sister Denis Radley, 1982–5
9. Sister Thomas Williams, 1985–91
10. Sister Magdalen Ingram, 1991–2
11. Sister Barbara Barry, 1992–

HEADMISTRESSES

1. Mother Veronica Lund, 1885–91
2. Mother Gertrude Blagden, 1891–8
3. Mother Barbara Hewett, 1898–1904
4. Mother Cecilia Marshall, 1904–21
5. Mother Ignatius Beveridge, 1921–49
6. Mother Mercedes Lawler, 1949–56
7. Mother Bridget Geoffrey-Smith, 1956–76
8. Sister Emmanuel Orchard, 1976–82
9. Sister Mark Orchard, 1982--
10. Mrs Rhian Amery, acting Headmistress, 1993–4

Sister Bridget maintains, and Sister Pia agrees with her, that it is more accurate to regard the first "Headmistresses" as "Sisters in charge". There were only twenty or so girls, and in any case the Superior was always the Principal of the school until recent times. (From 1913, Mother M. Ignatius is described as "Form Mistress and Mistress of Discipline". I take this to mean that she was in fact deputy Head, and indeed she did succeed to the post.) The transition from "Mother" to "Sister" is obvious; the beginning of the end of using adopted names in religion can also be seen. For example, Sister Denis is now Sister Armine. The practice of always being called Mary, both after Our Lady and Mary Ward, is beginning to slip, although the Sisters still include it in the vow formula.

Books and Articles Consulted

Bettenson H., *Documents of the Christian Church*, 2nd edn., OUP, 1963.

Bogan P., *Beloved Chapel: Milner's Church in Winchester*, published locally, 1988.

Bossy J., *The English Catholic Community, 1570 to 1850*, Darton, Longman and Todd, 1975.

Butler, Abbot Cuthbert, OSB, *The Life and Times of Bishop Ullathorne*, two volumes, Burns, Oates and Washbourne, 1926.

ibid. ed., *The Vatican Council, 1869 to 1870; The Letters of Bishop Ullathorne*, Fontana, 1962.

Caraman Philip, SJ, *Margaret Clitherow*, Catholic Truth Society.

Chambers, Mother Catherine, IBVM, *The Life of Mary Ward*, two volumes, Burns and Oates, 1882 and 1885.

Corbishley Thomas, SJ, *The Life of the Reverend Mother Cecilia Marshall, IBVM*, St George's Press, London, 1969.

The Dictionary of National Biography, Articles on Bishop White, Bishop Gardiner, Cardinal William Allen, Fr Robert Persons, SJ, Mary Ward.

Duffy Eamon, *The Stripping of the Altars: Traditional Religion in England, 1400 to 1580*, Yale University Press, 1992.

English Benedictine Congregation (various), *Consider Your Call*, SPCK, 1978.

ibid., *The English Benedictine Year Book, 1992*.

Fraser Antonia, *The Weaker Vessel*, Weidenfeld, 1984; Mandarin Paperback, 1992.

Gwynne D., *Lord Shrewsbury, Pugin and the Catholic Revival*, (with especial reference to introduction by Fr S. J. Gosling), Hollis and Carter, 1946.

IBVM Pamphlets, "The IBVM English Province, No 4: Errollston", privately circulated, 1992.

ibid., "What's Life Like in the Sixth Form?", published at Ascot, 1991.

Jamison Christopher, OSB, ed., "A School of the Lord's Service", papers presented at a seminar at Oxford, April 1985, on Spirituality in Catholic Boarding Schools, printed at Worth Abbey.

Ker I., *John Henry Newman, a Biography*, OUP, 1988.

King, Archbishop John Henry, *Hampshire and the Faith*, published locally, date unknown.

Mathew D., *Catholicism in England*, Eyre and Spottiswoode, 2nd edn., 1947.

Marshall, Reverend Mother Cecilia, unpublished letters to Mother Campion Davenport, Selected by Sister Mark Orchard.

Muir T. E., *History of Stonyhurst College, 1593–1993*, James and James, 1993.

Newman John Henry, "The Second Spring", a sermon preached on July 13th 1852, Catholic Truth Society.

Orchard, Sister Emmanuel/Gillian, IBVM, *Till God Will: Mary Ward through Her Writings*, Darton, Longman and Todd, 1985.

ibid., "Making Sense of Celibacy", special issue of *The Way*, Heythrop College, 1993.

ibid., "Journey into Freedom", essay in honour of the fourth centenary of the birth of Mary Ward, *The Way*, Heythrop College, 1985.

Southern R.W., *Western Society and the Church in the Middle Ages*, Pelican, 1970.

Sturman, Sister Mary Winifrede OSU, *The History of the Ursulines in England, 1851 to 1981*, Martell Press, Ramsgate, 1982.

Watkin E. I., *Roman Catholicism in England to 1950*, OUP, 1957.

Index